THE SPLIT SCREEN STRATEGY:

IMPROVEMENT + INNOVATION

THE SPLIT SCREEN STRATEGY:

IMPROVEMENT
+ INNOVATION

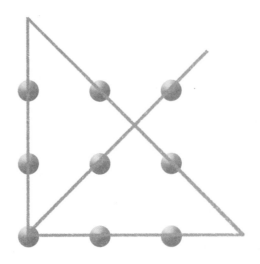

HOW TO GET EDUCATION CHANGING
THE WAY SUCCESSFUL SYSTEMS CHANGE

TED KOLDERIE

BEAVER'S
POND
PRESS

ISBN 13: 978-1-59298-928-7

Library of Congress Catalog Number: 2014907491

Printed in the United States of America

First Printing: 2014

18 17 16 15 14   5 4 3 2 1

Cover and interior design by James Monroe Design, LLC.

Beaver's Pond Press, Inc.
7108 Ohms Lane
Edina, MN 55439–2129
(952) 829-8818
www.BeaversPondPress.com

BEAVER'S
POND
PRESS

The e-book is available on the Amazon Kindle, Apple iBooks,
Barnes & Noble Nook, and Kobo.

"I realized that there was a very straightforward approach to solving the challenge.

"Not *having a background in structures was very helpful, because it permitted me more readily to adapt some very simple-minded techniques.* . . . *All the groups in England that were serious about this project had big teams of very qualified people that always included aircraft structural designers, and what they came up with were built like airplanes* . . . *They just adapted, very ingeniously, from standard aircraft structure techniques because that's what they knew and were comfortable with* . . .

"*When we tried to figure out why we succeeded when others didn't, it came down to a question of attitude* . . . *There is very little in our schools and our culture that forces us to get away from established patterns and to look at things in different ways* . . . *We need to be skeptical and try different routes to solve problems.*"

—Paul MacCready, Jr. in an interview
with the Yale Alumni Magazine.

MacCready was an aerospace engineer and inventor.
In June 1979, with his *Gossamer* aircraft, MacCready won the
Kremer prize for human-powered flight.

CONTENTS

PART THREE: IMPLEMENTING

PREFACE:

Sometimes things are 'too obvious'

When he found others failing to catch the essence of a problem, or unable to see the way out, a friend superbly skilled in public affairs used to say, "Some things are too obvious". Were he with us today he would, I believe, say that about the education policy discussion under way in this country.

His success in getting people to see things came from his being close enough to the situation to understand it yet independent enough of its politics to say what needed to be said. He had served in the Minnesota Legislature and had been legislative assistant to a congressman in Washington. A realist, he accepted that politicians need to get elected and need to respond to interest groups. Yet he could often find ways to get them to see the public interest as in their interest. He went to questions of structure because he understood how its incentives shape the way public bodies and public officials behave. His work was in real-time policymaking: Every session he was advising elected and appointed officials in local government and in the Legislature. Appreciating the power of proposals, he was always on the initiative, often re-setting the terms of the debate. "More change comes from challenge than from consensus," he would say.

The list of things "too obvious" in America's discussion about improving school and learning really is quite astonishing. Motivation must matter: Why is it not made central? Surely education is not really 'delivered' to students, is it—as if 'to learn' were a transitive verb. If we want better people in teaching why not work to make teaching a better job for its people? *Can* we discuss teaching without considering the way digital electronics are changing learning? Don't we need to consider that the behavior of teachers and their unions might be the predictable and rational consequence of the role assigned to teachers?

Perhaps most puzzling is that education policy continues to pursue what has been an unsuccessful theory of change. Why is the effort still to drive changes and improvements into an inert system rather than to change what makes K-12 an inert system? Most of our major systems use a different theory of change—and in some cases they change and improve dramatically; rapidly and without huge political conflict. *Why would the effort to transform education not adopt their successful theory of action?*

Let's begin there; with that need for a different approach to system-change.

INTRODUCTION

America can get itself better schools, better learning and a better education system. We've been going about the job the wrong way, blocked by an obsolete theory of action. We need to arrange for this system to change the way successful systems change.

It is time to give up the theory of action that looks toward a comprehensive transformation of the system, engineered politically.

The skills and knowledge of Americans are not what they need to be; the nation's system of education does need to be improved dramatically.[1] That much seems agreed. The issue is how. And in the discussion about education policy the 'how' has been shaped by two premises, not usually explicit so usually unquestioned.

The first is that there is somewhere a right model of school, a right approach to learning, which 'we must' identify and get everyone to agree on.

The second is that, with a consensus in place, 'policy' will then act 'comprehensively' to convert the system from the old model to the new.

It is the idea of starting with agreed-on goals and then working backward to develop and implement an orderly plan for change; basically the impulse toward centralization that Jal

---

1. "Torqued out", was the way Robert Astrup would privately describe the existing model, while president of the Minnesota Education Association. In first gear a car will go only so fast no matter how much gas you give it.

1

Mehta of Harvard in his book (of this title) calls "the allure of order". Or perhaps the preference for what Professor Charles Lindblom of Yale called "mechanisms of central authority". The dominant concept at any rate has been of some outside hand rearranging school and system—guided by data showing which of the things-now-being-done work best or by a desire to emulate what-they-do somewhere else. This preference for the comprehensive is visible in the way people test a new idea: Will it work everywhere?

This has not been a successful theory of action. The grand transformation never happens. There is no realistic possibility of its happening. The schemes advanced for transformation are sometimes quite elaborate—and radical: Commissioners of education, even, will occasionally say, "Blow up the system and start over". But people disagree about The One Best Way, for school and for system. So the needed consensus never develops. Even if it did, the comprehensive transformation could not be engineered. No state, and certainly not the national government, is going to "blow it up and start over". Nor can the political process handle the complexity involved in a plan that calls for implementing 27 changes over the succeeding nine years.

Still, calls for 'systemic reform' continue. A recent tendency has been to look abroad and to say, for example, that we should do what Finland does. But we cannot create the Finnish system here. In the first conversation Education|Evolving had with Pasi Sahlberg I asked: "When you began to design and install this new system after 1970 what was the role of the local authorities?" "Oh, none", he said. "Finland at that time was a totally centralized state." In America, where most schools belong to and are run by directly-elected independent special districts, the state cannot impose a radically different system free of the powerful politics of local consent. Nor could our national government impose such a radically different system on the states.[2]

---

2. *See* Chapter 11

Recognizing this, most of those concerned about some particular problem try to act specifically on that particular problem—leaving the larger system-structure unchanged. This is, in the narrow sense, realistic. If, for example, those concerned about the absence of standards and wanting to introduce standards had proposed at the same time to turn K-12 inside out and upside down, no one would have listened. So, being realistic, they accept the existing structure.

Problems, though, do not arise by themselves. Usually they are the symptoms of something in the underlying system-arrangements. Too often 'reform' attacks the visible symptoms of the problem, rather than working to remove whatever in the system is causing the problem. It is harder, of course, to change the basic system-architecture. And a lot of people do not want to go to the heart of the problem. So as the 'givens' remain, the problems remain. Year after year, decade after decade, what mainly emerges from the process is the incremental improvement of conventional school within the traditional system-arrangements.

With the desire for change humbled by the reality of what can be done, the education policy discussion is reduced to deploring problems and reaffirming goals; to talking endlessly about things not done that ought to be done, and about things being done that ought not to be done. Not surprisingly, people become discouraged; over time become cynical about the possibility of significant change. Thirty years on from *A Nation At Risk*, there is widespread disappointment with the progress in improving American education. People sense we are 'stuck'.

Not so. At least we do not *have* to be stuck. The country does not have to settle for endless incrementalism. This is one of those problems that is at its heart simple. The inability to change everything at once, the failure of 'systemic' reform, does not commit us eternally to the traditional system givens. We simply need to give up the effort to act 'comprehensively'. We need a different theory of system-change.

We need to examine and to understand the way successful systems change and to ask, "Why don't we arrange for education to change like that?"

Can it be done?

"Impractical", many will say about so dramatic a departure from conventional theory. But arranging for K-12 to change the way successful systems change *is the practical* theory of action. It is the conventional strategy that is *im*practical.

We could now make this fundamental turn in strategy; in our theory of action. All around us we see visible evidence of the way successful systems change. We need simply to bring that understanding into our thinking about education.

Bob Schwartz at Harvard talks about "multiple pathways". Ron Wolk, the founding editor of Education Week, talks in terms of "parallel tracks"—and in *Wasting Minds* in 2011 explained why.

That is almost our concept in this book, but not quite. What follows will argue for the multiple pathways or parallel tracks not to create a dual system but *as the process of system change in public education;* introducing innovation and using its dynamics to produce different and better schools and to transform K-12 into a self-improving system.

Here is the plan this argument will follow.

Part 1: Strategizing

Chapter 1: "Changing the way successful systems change" means running two efforts in parallel: opening to new and fundamentally different models while continuing to improve the traditional model. Think of it as a 'split screen' strategy, combining Innovation with Improvement.

Chapter 2: Chartering was introduced to provide the opening for innovation; to let public education generate new schools with different approaches to learning. But about 2004 it was turned to raising scores in traditional school. Now chartering should return to its focus on innovation.

Chapter 3: Innovation is harder for the district sector, accustomed as it is to making marginal improvements within the givens of traditional school. But there are ways for states to prompt the innovation the districts would not do if left on their own.

Part 2: Innovating

Chapter 4: Innovation is people trying things. The schools and teachers opting into the innovation sector will have the freedom to depart from any or all of the givens of the traditional K-12 arrangement.

Chapter 5: Maximizing motivation should be an early focus of the effort at innovation. This country could be getting a lot more than it is from both its students and its teachers. But—for both—excellence requires effort and effort requires motivation.

Chapter 6: Schools in the innovation sector will broaden both the range of subjects studied and the notion of student performance. Today's constricted concept of 'achievement' works to narrow what's studied. Higher achievement probably depends on broadening the concept of 'learning'.

Chapter 7: We could improve the achievement of teen-agers if we would modify the old institution of adolescence –that 'artificial extension of childhood' that holds young people back from doing all they can do. In their interest and in the country's interest we should challenge them harder and ask them to take more responsibility for their learning.

Chapter 8: The digital electronics now revolutionizing the handling of information are bound to transform school and learning. Initially the response is to 'blend' digital into traditional school. To realize its full potential there will need to be schools able to put 'digital' to non-traditional use, personalizing learning.

Chapter 9: Conventional 'reform' sees itself improving teachers' effectiveness. Yet by diminishing their role it might have the opposite effect. As learning personalizes, teachers' role needs to enlarge. If teachers can control what matters for student success teachers will accept accountability for student success.

Part 3: Implementing

Chapter 10: The innovation, the new and different approaches to learning and models of school, will come from the bottom up—as schools in both the chartered and the district sectors fight for autonomy. It will be an unorthodox process of change. But some powerful forces will be supporting it.

Chapter 11: Begin with the understanding that the states do not run the schools and that Washington cannot structure the K-12 system in the states. For state and national policymakers the key to change will be leadership and persuasion.

Chapter 12: The time has come to remember the importance of always changing what is not a winning game

PART ONE

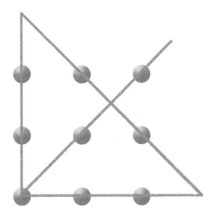

STRATEGIZING

CHAPTER 1

Move to a
'split screen' strategy

*"Changing the way successful systems change" means running
two efforts in parallel: opening to new and fundamentally
different models while continuing to improve the traditional
model. Think of it as a 'split screen' strategy, combining
Innovation with Improvement.*

Rather than trying to engineer a comprehensive system transformation the strategy for change will be to let fundamentally
different models come into education and let them spread gradually if and as they succeed.

This challenges the traditional strategy; the effort to drive
change through the system from the outside or from the top
down. But it is the practical strategy. Surely it is time at last to
be practical.

With this process of what Education|Evolving has called
"innovation-based systemic reform" the elementary/secondary
system can be transformed—perhaps fairly rapidly and with
minimal political conflict. Compare the results of innovation-
based systemic reform in, say, communications with the results
of standards-based systemic reform in K-12: In which system
has there been more change, more quickly?

The key is to open K-12 so schools and teachers can try things. This is harder than it sounds. The people wanting to try things are usually outside the mainline system, often people of little reputation. "Invention"—the term Professor Lienhard prefers—is essentially an "act of rebellion", and rebels are not welcomed. But those outside established organizations see what those inside do not; point out the need to challenge accepted wisdom and traditional practice.[3]

» In the 1930s, waiting to have his cargo of cotton unloaded from his truck—bale by bale—and loaded—bale by bale—into the hold of a cargo ship, a small-time trucker named Malcolm McLean wondered why it wouldn't be easier just to pick up the trailer from his semi and load that onto the ship. After 1945 he pursued that idea. Today 90 per cent of the world's trade in manufactured goods moves in containers.

» One summer in the 1950s a not-particularly-successful stockbroker—looking at the regulation that blocked small savers from the higher interest rates available to those able to buy large-denomination bonds—wondered what might happen if his firm bought large-denomination bonds and broke them into smaller units for sale to small savers. For some years the idea struggled for acceptance. But today the industry of money-market mutual funds is in the order of 2.5 trillion dollars.

» Working at Motorola in the early 1970s, Marty Cooper had the idea of taking the early two-way radio out of the automobile and turning it into a truly portable telephone. He fought for a decade with company officials who wanted him to make a better carphone. But in

---

3. See *How Invention Begins*. John H. Lienhard is an emeritus professor of mechanical engineering and history at the University of Houston and has been an essayist on National Public Radio.

1983 Motorola put the first cellphone on the market. It weighed a pound and sold for $4,000. He kept working to get the size down; to get the price down. Today over half the people in the world carry cellphones.

Clayton Christensen has made famous the distinction between the "sustaining innovation" that routinely improves (or reduces the cost of) existing products or business models and the "disruptive innovation" that introduces a business model or product model not on offer by existing producers. He explains why existing organizations are unable to disrupt themselves.

Traditional education policy produces sustaining innovation. Education needs an element of disruptive innovation.

Usually the disruptive innovation is not quality when it first appears. (Think about 'the first' anything.) Even so, early-adopters pick it up quickly. Adoption is voluntary: The idea is not to make all their users give up their land-line phones or their petroleum-powered automobiles, for example. Those who prefer the traditional may stay with the traditional. But those who stay with the traditional are not to suppress the innovative for those who do want that.

Existing organizations usually continue to improve the cost and quality of the traditional model. But the new and disruptive innovations also improve, sometimes rapidly. Over time, as the different gets better and as its price comes down, more people shift. At some point the curves cross. Ultimately the old might be closed out. The world's last typewriter factory has shut down; analog TV has gone dark. The incandescent light bulb might be dimming out.

We're all familiar with these transitions: canal boats and riverboats giving way to railroads, then railroads giving way to automobiles . . . personal computers replacing mainframe computers and typewriters . . . wind power and solar power now beginning to disrupt central-station electric power . . . department stores first unbundling into specialty stores and then giving way to discount stores . . . brick-box retail now being challenged by online retail. On and on.

The process is not without conflict. Organizations that do not change might disappear, so predictably they resist the different, sometimes politically. But it is through what Professor Charles Lindblom called this 'mechanism of mutual adjustment' that most systems progress, improve and are transformed.

Innovation-based change, in education

The idea for transforming education has, by contrast, been to move through what Lindblom called "mechanisms of central authority".

Public education developed as a governmental function (though in America largely separate from general local government). Over time it grew dramatically, first as 'high school' expanded to take in the children removed from work by the child-welfare laws and after that with the 'baby boom' that began in 1946. But it continued to be organized as a regulated public utility. And like most public utilities it lacked the dynamics to become a self-improving system.[4]

What change did appear in K-12 had to be forced in from the outside: desegregation after 1954, teacher-bargaining in the 1960s, special education in the 1970s. But these new features did not alter the basic structure of K-12. And they did not change schooling. The system was defended by its separation from general government at all levels and by its powerful ideology of 'local control'. While the executive of the National School Boards Association, Tom Shannon endlessly preached that "The school board is the foundation of American democracy". When it came

---

4. As the communications system evolved the model dominant at any given time also took the public-utility form; working at each stage to establish and maintain a monopoly. But each monopoly was disrupted as a new service appeared: telegraphy competing with the early postal service, then electric telegraphy competing with signals, then 'voice' telephony competing with Western Union. Professor Richard John described this process in Daedalus, Fall 1998.

to teaching and learning K-12 was a castle on a hill that policy-makers in general government did not enter.

For years this was a stable situation. The state created districts and districts created schools. School was free. You had to attend, but whether or not you learned was up to you: The state didn't care. You could tell it didn't, because it didn't check to see.

In the 1980s, however, the sense developed that knowledge was becoming the critical economic resource. The states did begin to test for learning. And K-12 issues began to open to outsiders. Ever since, the struggle has been to find the 'how'; the effective way to get school and learning to improve.

Notably, the strategy that appeared was not to turn public education into a self-improving system. The restructuring accepted that K-12 was an inert system. Efforts to increase financing, to lengthen day and year, to raise standards all accepted its traditional givens. The strategy was to drive-in these improvements with a combination of mandates and persuasion. 'Continuous improvement' is now coming to be the theory of action.

Not surprisingly, 'reform within the givens' . . . change that accepts the system features that make school so hard to change . . . has been only marginally effective; has produced only incremental improvements on the conventional model. The language in use exaggerates what actually happens: 'restructuring', 'reform', endlessly 're-', 're-', 're-'. The institution is skilled at giving the appearance of change.

The absurdity of this should have been obvious. Trying to drive change into an inert system requires more in the way of public energy and political capital, more time and money, than policy bodies and the local civic system can indefinitely sustain. A sensible strategy would focus on turning K-12 into a self-improving system, causing its organizations themselves to be continually in search of efficiency gains and quality improvements.

'Improvement-only' is an unacceptable risk

In addition to being questionable as a strategy, betting all the chips on continuous-improvement-only is indefensible politically and ethically. No one can be sure it will succeed. So it is a risk. It is not a necessary risk because we could at the same time be running an effort at innovation. *And because it is not a necessary risk to be taking it is not an acceptable risk to be taking, with the country's future and with other people's children.*

It is time to free our thinking about strategy from the 'one right way'; from the discussion about absolutes; from the wars about right-and-wrong, about 'this way or that way', about 'traditional' vs. 'progressive'. *It is time to run both improvement and innovation simultaneously, side by side.* This means doing in education what successful systems do; means opening to innovation.

This radically different 'split screen' strategy will challenge traditional education policy. It will distress researchers working to persuade policymakers they should take no action not based on data. (Data can hardly evaluate what has never been tried.) It will distress consultants who present as problems in the management of the organization what are in fact problems in the structuring of the industry. It will upset those who want change carefully controlled from the top so their solution might be *the* solution. It will be criticized by those impatient to see dramatic change quickly and by those who believe that only 'comprehensive' change can 'scale up' quickly.

But after four decades in which the one-bet strategy has produced only marginal change it is clear we need now to revive the old wisdom about changing a losing game. We need to get back to the common-sense wisdom that says: When in doubt try a number of different things.

Moving to a 'two-bet' strategy means opening education fully to innovation. From this starting-point the question is how, practically, to free up schools to innovate; requires clarifying what it means for them to adopt the new and different.

Let's think about that in the context of public education consisting now of both a district sector and a chartered sector.

Chartered sector first.

What do we mean by 'system' and 'system-change'?

This book proposes a different approach to 'system change'—which suggests that up front we should clarify what we mean by 'system'. 'System' does mean different things to different people. To a district superintendent 'system' means "My schools". We hear talk about "the New York school system" or "Chicago's school system". That's not our meaning here. The district is an organization.

In this book 'the system' will be the organizations all together; the districts and schools in this country; including now the schools in the chartered sector as well.

There's also the question what's meant by 'systemic'. People often talk—approvingly—about the need for change to be 'systemic'. To many people 'systemic' means 'comprehensive'; changing all the schools all at once, through some decisive policy action. In this book 'systemic' looks toward major change in the K-12 system but through a different process that starts with the definition I got from Paul Hill when he was with RAND. A system, he said, is "a collection of interacting parts". So 'systemic change' can mean altering just one of those 'parts' (or introducing some new part), generating dynamics that ripple through the system. As other parts respond, adjust, the entire system gradually changes. So it is not essential to act 'comprehensively' in order to produce a general, even radical, change.

Consider telecommunications. As microwave towers spread and as the communications satellite appeared the old industry based on 'long lines' changed dramatically. New competitors went after the long-distance traffic that generated the profits the Bell System used to subsidize local service. "They are driving us out of the price-averaging business", I heard the chief engineer of Northwestern Bell Telephone Co. say in the 1970s. The dynamics were powerful. In the end the CEO of AT&T decided to embrace deregulation and competition. Service changed, pricing changed, AT&T broke up. Then came the 'smartphone'.

Telecommunications has been transformed—but not through a comprehensive action engineered politically. Most large-scale change involves introducing some new dynamic into 'a collection of interacting parts', with change spreading gradually as existing elements adapt. That will be the concept of 'systemic change' in this book.

('System' can also refer to the principles on which an institution is organized. At times you'll see a reference to a 'public-utility system', for example. And in Chapter 3 we talk about a district moving from a 'bureau system' to a 'contract system'. I trust this won't prove confusing.)

CHAPTER 2

Create the 'space' for innovation

Chartering was introduced to provide the opening for innovation; to let public education generate new schools with different approaches to learning. But about 2004 it was turned to raising scores in traditional school. Now chartering should return to its focus on innovation.

Chartering was an *institutional* innovation, a redesign of the system-architecture of K-12; withdrawing the 'exclusive franchise' the state had previously given the districts, breaking up the old public-utility arrangement. The essential idea was to make it possible for some entity other than the district to start different public schools new, opening the way for innovation.

A rich discussion about education had begun in Minnesota after Jim Kelly arrived in 1981 to be president of Spring Hill Center, bringing with him his connections from his days with the education program of the Ford Foundation.

Through the 1980s Minnesota began gradually introducing choice into its system of public education. Much of that was due to Governor Rudy Perpich.[5] In 1983 he sought and got authority to name the commissioner of education. In 1984 the Berman/Weiler report to the Minnesota Business Partnership proposed public-school choice. In 1985 Perpich put the idea into the legislative session; got it through the education committees but saw it killed in the tax committee. That session did, however, enact the Post-Secondary Enrollment Option which let juniors and seniors finish high school in any Minnesota college or university. This carried the essential principle of chartering: some entity other than the local district offering public education. In 1988-89, Perpich having persisted, inter-district open enrollment came into law.

Choice among districts quickly stimulated a desire for more good schools for students to choose among. Discussion quickly focused on Albert Shanker's idea—floated at the National Press Club in Washington in April 1988—about teachers starting small schools. That was picked up and put under study by the Citizens League. That October Shanker presented it at the Minneapolis Foundation's Itasca Seminar. In the 1989 and 1990 legislative sessions (then) Senator Ember Reichgott championed the idea. It was enacted in 1991. Her account in *Zero Chance of Passage* is the best account of the origins of the legislation and of this breakthrough in the policy—and politics—of education.[6]

In 1990, in a paper titled "The States Will Have to Withdraw the Exclusive", I had offered a theory about what made K-12 an

---

5. Rudy Perpich was the eldest of four sons of immigrant Croatian parents, themselves with limited education. All four graduated from Hibbing High School on Minnesota's Iron Range. All four graduated from college. All four earned professional degrees. Three became dentists. All these went into the state senate. Rudy was elected lieutenant-governor in 1970 and succeeded to the governorship in 1977; lost in 1978; then was elected in his own right in 1982. The youngest son, Joe, became a psychiatrist and married the daughter of the publisher of the *New York Times*.

6. See http://www.zerochanceofpassage.com. Unknown to those in Minnesota—or elsewhere—Joe Loftus in Chicago, stimulated by the teachers' strike in 1987, had generated an almost identical proposal for the reform discussion there. Loftus shelved his plan when Chicago went instead for parent-run schools.

inert system.[7] Again, the problem was obvious: With its system of 'exclusive franchises' the state was assuring districts their economic success—whether or not they changed and improved and whether or not the students learned.

It was an arrangement that set all the wrong incentives. It had to be changed. And it was. After Minnesota's initial law in 1991 chartering spread rapidly. California's action in 1992 put the idea in play nationally. In 1993 six states acted. By 1998 about 40 states had chartering in some form. Everywhere these were 'state capitol policy initiatives'; remarkably bipartisan actions by legislators and governors, passing, in defiance of all conventional political reality, against the almost unanimous opposition of the major education associations. The chartered schools, though not themselves governmental, became part of the state's program of public education.

Legislators intended chartering to introduce both innovation and accountability.

The laws left it open as to the kind of school to be created. Pedagogically a 'charter school' was not a kind of school. 'To charter' was a verb; the new schools created were 'chartered schools'. Nor did the laws create schools: Teachers and others created schools, in a remarkable outpouring of interest, commitment and hard work testifying to the latent desire for something different and better.

The laws created a sector fundamentally different from the bureau model in the district sector of public education, where accountability is entrusted to management and to politics. Chartered schools were to be independent entities on contract to districts or to the state or entities designated by the state. What Minnesota initially called 'outcome-based' schools would be approved to operate for a defined term, renewal conditioned on their and their students' success.

---

7. See Appendix 3.

The new sector grew rapidly and quickly began to evolve. Caps were lifted or eliminated. New concepts of school and of sponsors (now called 'authorizers') appeared. Some organizations that had been creating schools in the private sector came into the new public sector, as did some that had been waiting for vouchers and some that had been trying to negotiate with districts for contracts.

Chartering did not, however, become the dominant strategy for change. In 1991 another strategy appeared: *standards*-based systemic reform. Unlike chartering, the 'standards' strategy was aimed at all schools, at existing schools. Promising to be 'systemic' it came on with far more influential policy and political support. Most important, it did not propose to upset the traditional arrangements in K-12. So 'standards' became the mainline strategy for change and improvement.

Chartering's attention to innovation faded

Much might have been different had researchers and the media focused on the kinds of chartered schools being created; on the innovation appearing. In fact the opposite happened. This was partly because the language changed. The verb forms— chartering, to charter, chartered—fell away. As schools appeared 'charter' quickly became an adjective. The talk about 'charter schools' implied these were a kind of school.

Many of the schools created were, in truth, not innovative. For many people organizing schools the object was mainly to get outside the district bureaucracy and outside the union contract.

But there has been more innovation in the chartered sector than most people recognize. It was not picked up, however, in the education research which pays little attention to single cases of new-and-different. Few researchers looked to see what any particular school was as a school; what it had its students reading, seeing, hearing and doing. As John Witte from the University of Wisconsin explained at the American Education Research Association in 2003, research looks to generalize, looks for 'measures of central tendency'; for 'most' and 'on balance' and 'overall' and 'by and large'. Nor did the media get a clear view of the innovation and its significance.[8]

With no one looking to see what the schools in fact had their students reading, seeing, hearing and doing, the discussion was left with only the distinction between 'charter' and 'district'. And after the No Child Left Behind legislation in 2001 ratcheted up 'accountability', the question was: In which sector do students score higher on the state assessments in English and math?

What passed for research tried simply to link 'charter' to learning. Advocates pointed to studies showing 'charter schools' scoring higher than district schools; opponents pointed to studies showing them scoring less well or no better. Given the differences among schools in each sector most studies came back saying, "The evidence is mixed"—as of course it would be. It was an unproductive discussion; roughly the equivalent of debating whether eating-out is better than eating-in.

There was also, of course, the conflict bound to be generated by so disruptive a system-innovation. Some of that was ideological, extending the political argument over 'choice' that had come with inter-district enrollment. Much of it was interest-based, some of that from districts trying to persuade policymakers that the new schools would be "taking *our* money".

Predictably perhaps, a new effort appeared in 2004 aimed at defending and advancing the new sector by ensuring that 'charter schools' *would* do better than district schools; scoring higher and demonstrating that the chartered sector would enforce accountability in a way the district sector could not. Not much has been written about this development by journalists or by researchers.

---

8. When the two brothers from Dayton, Ohio sent word back to the local newspaper they had flown their 'airplane' 120 yards the editor put the story on the spike: Who cares? Equally, research looking to generalize would have dismissed the event: The preponderance of evidence would still have shown that most heavier-than-air craft cannot fly. But what difference did that 'most' make once Wilbur and Orville had got it right?

It is worth setting down what I know about what happened, how it happened and why.

Foundations create a new 'leadership organization'

During the first decade of chartering the state associations and their support groups had become loosely linked through the Charter Friends National Network (CFNN), created in Minnesota about 1996 with help from the Challenge Foundation and others. CFNN was not an organization but a project connecting the state-based organizations. Concurrently, at the Center for Education Reform in Washington, Jeanne Allen was keeping a nationwide inventory of the schools and the laws. Basically, though, there was no national entity to advocate for the sector; to explain, defend and interpret it.

Discussion began about creating a formal national organization to support and advance chartering through federal and state policy changes and stronger state advocacy organizations. What initially appeared in March 2003 was the National Charter School Alliance, a membership organization with a blend of state association people and national advocates who would be elected to its governing board by the state-based membership. Howard Fuller became its chair. Dean Millot, earlier with RAND, became its executive and began to set up a Washington-based office and staff.

In the summer of 2003 several foundations active in the financing of new schools—including some that had supported CFNN—expressed a desire for a 'leadership organization' rather than a membership organization. This thinking crystallized at a donors' strategy session July 17 at Charlottesville, Virginia, just prior to a meeting of charter actives called by the Progressive Policy Institute. It developed further at a second meeting in early August in Philadelphia. The sense was, as one consultant privately put it, that for chartering to realize its potential "the little people" needed to give way and be replaced by "the heavy hitters".

The foundations decided not to provide financing for the initial design. The organization was dissolved. Staff were let go. Fuller appointed a group of board members to come up with a new design acceptable to the funders. That took another year. In October 2004 the National Alliance for Public Charter Schools appeared as the new Washington-based national leadership organization. Nelson Smith was brought in to be its executive. The foundation money then arrived.[9]

Over the next several years a number of existing state and local charter support organizations—as in California and Washington DC—were de-funded. 'Strategic planning' grants became available to organizations willing to fall in with the new initiative. By March 2008 most of the early state-based members had been removed from the Alliance board.

The push for high-scoring schools

With the leadership organization established the next challenge was to establish a rationale and strategy for the reconceived chartered sector. This emerged from a task force created by the Alliance's new executive. Its January 2005 report was presented to a meeting of the charter family that Smith called for Mackinac Island the following August.

The thrust of "Restoring the Compact" was to establish that chartering was about accountability for achievement conventionally defined. The idea was to zero in on what was seen as the nation's most conspicuous failure—the low levels of achievement among low-income and minority children in the big-city districts—and to build the chartered sector by demonstrating

---

9. The name was unskillful, the use of 'public' to modify 'charter' suggesting there might also be private charter schools. To make its point that public education now has both a district and a non-district sector the organization should have called itself the National Alliance for Charter Public Schools.

that it could produce schools able to meet that challenge and to close schools that did not.

Schools with students scoring high on the state assessments were described as "quality charters"—despite the cautions of statisticians that student proficiency scores cannot be taken as a measure of *school* quality. Interest was low in any other dimension of achievement.[10]

Early in 2012, after Nelson Smith's resignation and during the tenure of an interim executive, the Alliance conducted a further round of strategic planning. It recommended phasing-down further the role of, and support for, the state-level work and state support organizations. More emphasis would go to growing the number of 'high-performing charters' and CMOs.

Strong efforts appeared to grow the sector, to 'scale up'. The idea was to create as quickly as possible a fairly small number of organizations operating networks of schools designed to produce high scores. These came to be called Charter Management Organizations (CMOs). Single-unit, freestanding schools were disparaged as "mom and pop" schools.[11] Foundations focused their grant-making on CMOs, and pressed the U.S. Department of Education to give preference to CMO networks in its grants for the start-up of new schools. A $50 million set-aside has been created for grants to multi-state CMO networks.

On the 20th anniversary of the first chartered school opening, the Alliance, meeting in Minnesota, released "Fulfilling the Compact". Later in 2012 the Progressive Policy Institute issued "Improving Charter School Accountability".

Everything now focuses on creating schools that do produce high scores ('high-performing schools') and on closing schools that do not ('failing schools'). State legislatures are urged to

---

10. See Stephen Raudenbush's 2004 Angoff lecture for the Educational Testing Service at http://www.etx.org/research/policy_research_reports/publications/publication/2004/curg. "Equating percentage-proficient with school quality", Raudenbush said, "cannot withstand serious scientific scrutiny".

11. Though these independent schools still dominate the chartered sector.

make achievement on the state assessments of English and math the basis for approving a new charter and for renewing an existing charter.

More and more the effort seems to be moving through the National Association of Charter School Authorizers (NACSA), an organization with broadly the same backers as the Alliance but with an agenda focused more directly on state rules that affect which schools open and which schools close. In late November 2012 NACSA announced a "One Million Lives" campaign, aiming over the coming five years to close 1,000 'low-performing' schools and to open 3,000 'quality' schools serving one million students. NACSA wants states to make renewal contingent on high scores (not just progress toward higher scores). It wants a single statewide authorizing body, of the sort enacted earlier in Arizona and most recently in Washington State and in Georgia. In April 2014 the Alliance joined NACSA in urging states to enact laws requiring the automatic closure of 'low-performing' schools.

There is strong disapproval of the pressures that make it difficult to close low-scoring schools. There is little sympathy for parents trying to keep open a school that has been good for their daughter, pleading that its closure will mean her returning to a district school admittedly worse. The attitude is: "Sorry about your problem, but my job is to close failing charters." The idea is that authorizers that do not close low-scoring schools should themselves be terminated.

'Our post-district future'

The effort is highly organized. A group of major foundations finances the key national organizations. Increasingly in major cities philanthropy is being organized to support the effort to produce 'high-performing schools'. The reform effort has been able to broaden politically (Democrats for Education Reform) and to draw in younger people (Students for Education Reform) and to attract some in teaching (the Association of American Educators) and those focused on higher standards and conventional reform generally (50CAN, StudentsFirst and others).

Results have been remarkable. The intense focus on improving the performance of elementary students in the inner cities has attracted resources to support the start-up and expansion of schools. Donors are thrilled to see young children in schools that look and feel like real school; serious school. And as the chartered sector has grown in some of the nation's largest or most troubled cities donors also sense they are at last getting American public education right.

There is now a fairly clear intent to convert big-city public education from the district model to this "high-performing" charter model. "The replacement scenario", Jal Mehta calls it, in *The Futures of School Reform,* his report from the project organized by the Harvard Graduate School of Education. Around the country there is now talk of "our post-district future".

The Alliance now keeps track of the changing market share of district and charter in the cities: Washington DC, New Orleans, Philadelphia and others.[12] The need for replacement is obvious, some advocates say, because there is in America no 'high-performing' urban district; not one. "Districts on the Decline" was the lead article in the Winter 2013 issue of The School Choice Advocate, the newsletter of the Friedman Foundation for Educational Choice. With fewer districts available (about 40,000 in 1961; about 13,000 today) Americans now must look increasingly to choices outside the district system, it said.

The effort continues: to attract financial support, to ally with important city, state and national political leadership, to attract and develop talent—teachers and others, to acquire facilities, to move state and national policy to support the growth of CMO networks and to install an accountability system keyed on test results. It is impressive. And important.

---

12. See the NAPCS 2013 "Market Share" report.

At the same time, those in the effort remain conscious of the obstacles; their challenges. As district schools close in some cities opposition rises in inner-city neighborhoods. The closings might result from the district's own financial, personnel or pension problems, but it is easy for opponents to blame 'charters'. There is an awareness that the movement does not look enough like the people it aims to serve: Race matters, in inner cities. Howard Fuller continues to suggest it would help if those in charge would come out in favor of at least some of the rest of the inner-city agenda: housing, income support, health care, social services.

An important disagreement exists about how to relate to the district sector: Is it better, strategically, for the chartered sector to separate itself as clearly as possible from the 'failing' district schools? Or should it work to persuade districts to adopt the new model; to have a chartered sector, in effect, inside the district? There appear also to be differences developing about how to define quality; performance; success.

Where is the R&D sector for public education?

There is an even more fundamental strategic question facing the sector, however, raised by its drift away from the idea of using chartering as a strategy for innovation.

Clearly the public is interested in what happens: Most people are not much interested in 'theories of action', 'strategy' and 'policy'. So it has been realistic in a sense for those controlling the sector to focus on the sort of schools that appear and on how well the students score. But the effect has been to turn the chartered sector into an effort to improve traditional school—at the elementary level: Far too little is said about high school. There is an interest in digital technology, visible in the photos of the schools. But as Michael Horn of the Clayton Christensen Institute concedes, this is 'sustaining innovation'. Its potential is to personalize, but in these schools 'blended learning' is captive to age-grading.[13]

Innovation is critical for the success of American education, and chartering remains the states' and the nation's best strategy for innovation—for introducing, quickly, the new approaches to learning now possible. *Innovation is chartering's comparative advantage.* And strategy matters.

In the summer of 2012 Nina Rees came in as the Alliance's new executive. In her first year she was clearly willing to listen to some different and dissenting voices. Lisa Graham Keegan, chair of NACSA, in her recent testimony to Congress, spoke favorably of innovation. Whether any of this means a modification of the essential strategy adopted in 2005 is not yet clear. It seems reasonable to believe a major adjustment in the thinking of its backers would be required for the Alliance itself to return to an emphasis on innovation.

This leaves the strategic question: Why would those now leading the chartered sector dismiss the opportunity it offers, to capture the future?

Interestingly, a similar question arises for the district sector, as it sees itself threatened in the major cities. And for state policy leadership.

Were chartering to fail . . . were there no longer a 'somebody else' to spur change . . . state leadership would find itself back where it was before 1991, confronted again by a public-utility system resistant to change.[14] *Why would governors and legislatures want to do that?*

With their superior resources the districts might be able to match the chartered sector in doing conventional school better. And they might find ways to develop an innovation sector internally, with schools that offer teachers broader roles and respon-

---

13. See Chapter 8.
14. See Appendix 3.

sibilities.[15] If they wish the states can—certainly have the capacity to—drive these responses in the district sector with a major institutional innovation comparable to chartering.

Let's look at that possibility. With K-12 having both a district sector and a chartered sector, with improvement and innovation running together, we are seeing the split screen strategy in operation.

---

15. See Chapter 9

CHAPTER 3

A state can stimulate its districts to act

Innovation is harder for the district sector,
accustomed as it is to making marginal improvements within
the givens of traditional school. But there are ways for states
to prompt the innovation the districts would not do if left on
their own.

The idea of replacing the traditional school district in major cities is not wholly without merit. It is not immediately obvious it is a sound principle that there can be only one organization offering public education in a city *no matter how large.*

For all its great contributions to education in this country, the American school district is a troubled institution.

The board of education sits in a conflict of interest. At election time it tells the public that it will get the children 'the best possible education'. Not quite. Not often does a board search widely around the country to bring in a portfolio of learning models to serve the differing needs of the children it enrolls. Typically it puts the children into the schools of an organization it owns and runs, in which its members serve as the directors and officers.

The reality of this self-dealing arrangement is seldom put directly. But I got no criticism when I wrote in the 1990 memo:

"Our system of public education is a bad system. It is terribly inequitable; it does not meet the nation's needs; it exploits teachers' altruism; it hurts students. It is unproductive and unfair to put people under incentives that are not aligned with the mission they have been given to perform".

Today the 'exclusive franchise' arrangement that let the district "take its customers for granted"—as Albert Shanker put it at the Itasca Seminar in 1988—has been withdrawn to some degree in most states. Still, the district sector retains much of the old culture. The impulse is still to appeal for loyalty to the old concepts, to plead for additional resources and to restrain those in other sectors who are moving faster to make change. Slow to accept the appearance of choice, boards and central office administrators still talk as if the children in the community belong to them; as if the revenue belongs to them rather than to the taxpayers and to the students.

Trying to 'look legitimate', districts cling to traditional arrangements; to what Mary Metz at the University of Wisconsin calls "real school". They remain hostile to chartering. They find it hard to create new schools—even their own—that would draw students away from existing schools. The typical district will do one of almost everything it senses is popular. But districts are reluctant to let even the successful 'different' spread. Some districts point with pride to their waiting lists.

Today's pressure for 'accountability' reinforces the district's impulse to centralize. Boards and central offices feel they must double down on what will produce high scores. They ask what works, then direct their schools to do what the consultants recommend. The sense of being responsible makes them reluctant to delegate authority. "We're the ones who run the schools", said the president of the National School Boards Association when Anne Bryant was appointed its executive director. It is telling that in the states the association of superintendents usually calls itself the association of "school administrators".

Yet some progressive superintendents are now visibly inter-ested in different arrangements. These are superintendents who see the districts losing students, who understand that students have choices and who see the problem of trying to standardize school and learning in a high-choice environment. In some cases where teachers come to them, asking to do-different—outside, in the chartered sector—these superintendents respond by offering the teachers the chance to set up their new school within the district.[16]

But this response does not have to be left to the initiative of individual districts. *If the district sector proves slow to move on its own to innovate, the state as the system architect for K-12 could intervene to introduce dynamics for change and innovation.*

Divestiture

Too often administrators at the state level talk as if they can do nothing without the power to command. Legislators are not so constrained. And legislatures have a duty to act. I remember saying to a group of state legislators, at the Harvard Graduate School of Education in 1993, that the problems in K-12 are not the boards' fault, not the teachers' fault, not the unions' fault. "They're your fault. The boards and teachers and unions did not make the system. The legislature made this system. It's up to the legislature to remake it."

The legislators' job is not to run the schools. Their job is to create a workable system for those who do. The 1990 memo said: "The state owes boards, teachers and administrators—and the public—a system in which those who do change and improve are supported and rewarded and in which those who do not are the ones put at risk. Everywhere in this country the state is in default on that obligation."

---

16. See page 103.

The state could now discharge that obligation in much the same way state policymakers introduced chartering to remove the districts' 'exclusive' on public education. State legislatures could again 'throw a lightning bolt' that would maximize the prospect of the districts giving schools real capacity to change. Call this *divestiture*.[17]

Essentially a legislature would, at least in certain districts, end the self-dealing arrangement by removing the board from its operating role, requiring it to bring in 'somebody else' to run the schools. Divestiture would drop the bureau arrangement and in its place insert a contract arrangement.

Divested of its operating control of the schools the board would have to focus on the policy questions: What are the learning needs? What do we want students to know? Who will we bring in to do the work? How well is the job coming? What do we do if the job is going well or not well?

The superintendent would no longer be a 'school administrator'. The role of the urban superintendent would revert to the role of the old county superintendent of schools: *to oversee the quality of education in schools s/he did not own and run.*

Here are the main outlines of a divestiture plan that might serve as a response to the attack on big urban districts.

» **Be selective.** The state might introduce divestiture only for districts of a certain size, or only for districts failing to make acceptable progress with learning, or only for those showing inadequate interest in change.

» **Use divestiture to reduce scale,** breaking *down* a large city school administration without breaking *up* the district geographically. For too long the notion has been that in a reorganization the scale of the policy side and the scale of the operating side must move together. That means a consolidation enlarging the district for

---

17. Most of what follows is drawn from the 1990 memo.

taxing purpose also enlarges the schools; an outcome many resist. Conversely, an effort to preserve small schools would preserve the small taxing jurisdictions; carrying forward the social and economic disparities that most everyone finds politically objectionable. Better options appear when we see the scale of policy and of operations changing separately.

John Maas proposed a version of this when executive director of the superintendents' association in Minnesota in the mid-1970s.

Influential legislators were pushing at the time for conventional consolidation, which meant merging the district administrations as it created a larger entity for policy and fiscal purposes. Clearly this was unhealthy for superintendents' careers.

Maas and key superintendents suggested: Consolidate only the policy side; retain the several existing operating organizations. He would point to the four suburban districts in north Ramsey County: Roseville, Mounds View, North Saint Paul and White Bear Lake.

Create a single jurisdiction with a stronger tax base and a single elected board.

Leave the four existing operating administrations, each contracted to the new board.

Have each of the four administrations operate schools in all parts of the new consolidated district, giving parents in each neighborhood some choice among different organizations with different approaches to learning.

» **Give the targeted districts a first chance to draw the divestiture plan themselves.** The legislation could give each district selected for divestiture a year, say, to adopt a divestiture plan of its own design. Only if the local district did not act would a state plan be imposed. Given the choice the selected district might well prefer to write its own plan.

» **In the state plan, offer options to the districts.**

* The board of education might spin off its entire 'school administration' into a single public operating corporation and have a sole-source contract with that.

* At the other extreme a board might contract separately with each school; creating something like 'a charter district'.

* Equally, a board might line up its schools and count off by threes, forming a Gold group, a Silver group and a Bronze group; then contract with each.

» **Let each contracted entity select its own mode of operation.** One might elect to centralize; another might delegate authority to its schools. One or more might prefer conventional instruction; others might choose non-traditional learning, personalized or project-based.

Pushed away from the traditional fire-department model by divestiture, a district would have incentives—reasons and opportunities—to consider the split screen model; to have at least one of its contracted operators moving to an innovation model. With a divestiture plan a district could come to resemble the chartered sector in its capacity to introduce different approaches to learning.

Boards divested of their operating responsibilities would have vastly more influence over the learning program than they have today: to diversify it, to change it and to hold its operators accountable.

What innovation?

Having looked at chartering and divestiture as ways to create the opportunity to do-different, it is time now to turn to what 'different' might mean.

What follows in Part Two walks a difficult line. Please understand that the idea is not to specify a model to be used by all schools. Rather, see chapters 4 through 9 as setting out the 'givens' in traditional school *from which the schools on the innovation side of the split screen will be free to depart.*

The core idea is to give schools the freedom to come up with approaches to learning and forms of school not currently in use—even not currently known. The definition of innovation will be *letting people try things.*

PART TWO

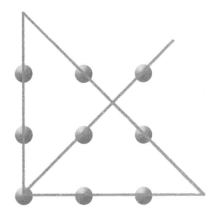

INNOVATING

CHAPTER 4

It's all right for some to 'do different'

Innovation is people trying things.
The schools and teachers opting into the innovation sector will
have the freedom to depart from any or all of the givens of the
traditional K-12 arrangement.

It can't be said too often: The split screen strategy is a fundamental departure from what has been the conventional thinking about the process of system change. It steps outside the argument about right and wrong; good and bad. No more effort to make schools be all like this or all like that. Rather, there'll be parallel efforts running at continuous improvement and at innovation.

> » On the improvement side the default strategy will
> continue; the effort to implement the new standards and
> assessments; scores as the measure of student learning;
> districts if they wish centralizing and standardizing
> their schools' and teachers' instruction for those who
> want that. The traditional givens about place and time,
> about age-grading and about whole-class instruction
> will remain, largely unquestioned. Most schools in the
> district sector, and the CMO schools in the chartered
> sector, will still be about conventional achievement.

> » On the innovation side of the split screen truly
> autonomous schools will continue to appear; schools

in which teachers will be able to shape the learning program in ways they believe will best serve their students; replicating what they've seen other schools doing successfully or, if they wish, trying things not tried before. In the district sector these innovative schools will be those operating under 'site-based' or 'self-governed' legislation or within an 'innovation zone' program like that recently enacted in Minnesota. In the chartered sector they will likely be the single-unit, free-standing, schools able to make independent decisions about their approach to learning and their form of organization.

"Letting people try things" means freeing them from the assumptions that:

» **School is a place, a building,** to which children come at set times of day, week and year.

» **Students are sorted by age** and move up the grades a year at a time. Secondary school usually runs through age 18. Attendance is mandatory usually through age 16, though in some states the leaving-age is now being raised.

» **The teacher is the worker** on the job of learning; that the technology is teacher-instruction and that education is something adults do to young people.

» **The work is mainly "batch processing",** as Ted Sizer used to say; group work in class-rooms.

» **Teachers are employees and work for an administrator** who is in charge of the school. The school is a unit of the district, not autonomous.

» **'Professional issues' are reserved to management.** Teaching is not a professional career.

In the innovation sector schools can also be smaller—as most all schools in the chartered sector have been from the start. This in contrast to the district sector, where schools are large and have been growing larger—a change not always made in the student interest.[18]

Size matters because it affects school culture. I remember a session of a Chamber of Commerce program organized to give young business people a look into various corners of local government. This day it was education. The presenter was an assistant principal at a 1,200-student middle school in a low-income neighborhood of Saint Paul.

His stories had his listeners cowering in their seats; probably were intended to make them think, "These educators have a really tough job. They need all the support we can give them". It was about unruly classrooms, fighting in the hallways, about students disturbing class in ways that stunned the group. When he finished someone asked: "If you were in charge of this district would you have a school that large in a neighborhood like that?" Immediately he said, "No. Of course not". Then everyone thought about that for a while.

What will it mean to depart from the givens?

Today everyone talks about innovation: Who *doesn't* want to be thought innovative? So like most terms that become so popular, 'innovation' has lost most of its meaning. It now means any change whatsoever; not something new anywhere but some-

---

18. Around the Twin Cities area many three-grade high schools have more than 2,500 students. "When I came this district had nine schools", a superintendent in a fairly small Twin Cities suburban district said to me once. "When I leave it will have three."

thing new *here*, however long known elsewhere. People say 'innovation' but mean 'replication'.[19]

In an effort at real innovation schools on that side of the split screen will be able to break the givens. They will be able to challenge the assumptions about time of day, week and year, and to get away from grouping children by age in 'grades'; will be free to expand learning outside the building, can abandon the notion of education as "the teacher filling the child's empty head with knowledge" and will be able to shape truly professional roles for teachers.

'Being able' means not having to get explicit permission in advance.

Normally when the question of doing-different arises the impulse is to ask, "What *is* your innovation?" and to assume that some higher body will have to approve what the school proposes to do.

This is visible in some of what pass today as 'innovation statutes'. These usually set up a process that begins by asking teachers to get approval from their principal; then for the school to get permission from its district; then for the district to get permission from the state. As the proposal climbs the ladder the questions are: "Has this been done before?" "Is there research that shows it works?" And, even if not explicit: "Will this upset anyone?"

It is hard for those 'in charge' to allow something dramatically different. They might find the proposal inconsistent with the planned-system-change they are working to implement. Or

---

19. Reporting on the November 2013 defeat of the tax-increase proposal for Colorado schools a New York Times reporter wrote that, had it passed, it would have "encouraged local innovations like longer school days and school years". In November 2013 the U.S. Department of Education gave its 'Investing in Innovation' awards to applicants that agreed to scale-up proven ideas for improving learning.

might feel it interferes with their control. They worry, too, about the risk in change: "What if . . . What if . . .?"[20]

Innovation does of course have givens and imperatives of its own. Those delegating autonomy to schools must:

» **Keep the scale of change small** so the failures, if any, will be small and can be quickly corrected.

» **Ensure the innovation schools are schools of choice.** Innovation cannot be imposed on the unwilling.

» **Arrange for the change so far as possible to be non-political.** As someone said, "If your innovation is controversial, don't put it to a vote".

» **Be realistic.** The new-and-different at the start will not be 'quality' as quality is currently defined. Give it time to improve. Usually it will; sometimes rapidly. Recognize, too, that it takes time for people to adjust to the 'different'. I remember a senior secretary who definitely did not want the new IBM Selectric typewriter—until she had used it a while.

» **Emphasize the risks in *not* innovating.** The existing system is riddled with risk and failure. Many children are, in the famous phrase, "left behind" today. This failure is not acceptable simply because it is familiar. Can you imagine this country tolerating in its other major systems—the airline system, say; or communications, electric-power-supply, food distribution, water-supply—the level of failure in K-12

---

20. People do fear what they have not seen before. Don Geesaman came from Blair, Nebraska, a town up the Missouri River from Omaha. Blair was small enough and rural enough that most back yards had gardens. At the Humphey School of Public Affairs in the 1980s Don used to tell a story that clearly had deep meaning for him. He said he went out one day and saw the lady next door flailing away with a hoe at something on the ground. He walked over and saw some poor animal quivering its last. "I didn't know what it was", she said to him. "So I killed it."

today? . . . the low levels of student proficiency, the high turnover of teachers, the slow take-up of the new digital electronics; the absence of growth in productivity.

The split screen strategy seems a reasonable strategy. Those vested in traditional ways can feel reassured: It removes the fear that comes with trying to change everything radically, all at once. Those who prefer traditional school may stay with traditional school. The 'different' will come in at the bottom rather than down from the top. Change will be voluntary; gradual.

CHAPTER 5

Innovate to generate motivation

*Maximizing motivation should be an early focus
of the effort at innovation. This country could be getting a lot
more than it is from both its students and its teachers. But—for
both—excellence requires effort and effort
requires motivation.*

The idea of making motivation a prime goal might surprise most people. People commonly say the goal is learning—and it is. But goals require strategies. School, teachers—and policymakers— have to find what *causes* learning.

For learning motivation matters. Motivating *students* matters, first of all. Students are co-workers on the job of learning. The old view survives, of the teacher as the worker, 'delivering education'. But results will improve when students want to learn.

When heading Public Agenda, Deborah Wadsworth cited Daniel Yankelovich's concept of "discretionary effort". There is, he said, a level of effort people will give you to keep their jobs. There is an additional level of effort they can give you if motivated to do so. Your job in managing organizations—and in designing organizations—is to elicit that discretionary effort.

You seldom hear 'motivation' in today's education policy discussion. Some people believe students will do better if school is more 'rigorous'.[21] More often 'standards' appears as the driver of learning. Listen to the discussion about the Common Core. Go on the websites of the organizations supporting and promoting it, and in the 'Search' box type the word 'ensure'. Look at, think about, what comes up. The assertion is almost literally that simply having standards will produce learning.[22]

So what motivates students?

In a long afternoon discussion with Education|Evolving in 1999 Jack Frymier laid out the case for making motivation central and explained what is required to do that. Frymier spent his career on the curriculum and instruction side; first as a teacher and administrator, then as a professor at Ohio State University for many years before moving to Phi Delta Kappa.

» Students learn when they're motivated to learn. If they want to learn, they will. If they don't, you probably can't make 'em. *Any successful effort to improve learning will therefore be fundamentally about improving students' motivation.*

» Motivation is individual. Young people differ; in personality, in background and experience, in sociability, in creativity, in intelligence, in their interests and aptitudes. Different students are motivated by different things. No effort at motivation will succeed unless it works with these differences.

---

21. You sometimes wonder if those who talk 'rigor' understand what it means. Merriam-Webster says: "harsh inflexibility; austerity; strictness, severity or cruelty; difficult, challenging, uncomfortable; strict precision, exactness."

22. In the business world such an assertion would be a 'forward-looking statement', of the sort a business corporation could not legally make without spelling out the risks that stand in the way of its strategy and its business plan succeeding. [In my mail recently came a typical annual report—in which the discussion of 'risk factors' takes up 15-pages of the 10-K report.

» 'School' is not very well tuned to the differences among students. Teachers might know students less well today than in the past. Schools are pressed now to be interested mainly in what students know and can do; less in who they are. Students move around; are moved around. Schools are age-graded: Students are with a teacher for a year; next year, have another. Schools are larger: As Ted Sizer has pointed out, high-school teachers especially have far too many students to know any of them well.

» Curriculum materials are not often adapted to individual students.

» Teaching methods are not often varied according to the needs and interests of the individual student. Some teachers do this, but many do not. Teachers work mostly with students in groups; most are obsessed with 'classroom management'. Most teachers talk too much (as Professor John Goodlad also reported from his research, in *A Place Called School*).

» Adapting materials and methods to individual student needs is a teachable skill. It just isn't very often taught where teachers are trained.

» Teachers aren't given much opportunity to modify 'instruction' in this way. The curriculum is 'sequenced'; teachers are not encouraged to modify the order in which things are taught, or how much time is spent on what. Students are not free to pursue a topic that interests them: The schedule calls for the course to move on.

» There are no rewards and few opportunities for teachers trying to modify teaching in this way, so that learning becomes interesting to the student and becomes the responsibility of the student.

» Because school takes this form most academic subjects are not of interest to most students. If it weren't for the extracurriculars there would be a revolution by young people in school.

So motivation does seem to matter. Yet how often do you hear those pushing for achievement talking about motivation? How many people do you know who would stand up to defend the proposition that traditional school, the American K-12 institution is designed . . . well designed, or consciously designed . . . to maximize student motivation? Would you, yourself?

Later I put Frymier's proposition to a key person in the 'standards' movement.

"I don't buy that', he said.

"Well, I asked, how will you get students to make the effort needed to meet the standards?"

He said, "There are a lot of people working very hard on that.

I persisted: "Who, for example?"

"Jim McPartland at Johns Hopkins", he said.

A few days later I called McPartland; put the question to him.

"Well", he said, "you have to start with motivation".

Motivation matters for teachers, too

No more than it can 'do' better learning can policy 'do' better teaching. So Yankelovich's wisdom about eliciting discretionary effort applies to teachers as well. Anything extra we can get from teachers would matter—and might be doubly important because the teacher's effort is key in eliciting that extra level of student effort.

Personalization and professionalization might be the key. Chapter 8 explains how digital electronics let teachers adapt to the differences in motivation they discover among their students. Chapter 9 explains how rearranging teachers' work and teachers' role can maximize teachers' opportunity to personalize learning and in the process motivate teachers.

Motivation matters for the economics of education, too. Teachers we pay; student effort we do not compensate. Whatever extra we get from students comes for free. This does seem to strengthen the case for a policy designed to elicit that discretionary effort from students. Why would a state wanting to improve learning and pressed on the revenue side—as most are—*not* want to maximize the contribution it gets from the workers it does not have to pay?

If maximizing motivation is obvious why is it so neglected?

Some believe it is wrong to begin with what interests students. They see this as a 'slippery slope' leading down to the dreaded constructivism. But there is also a curious resistance to incentives. Some feel that incentives are wrong in a system (presumably) driven by altruism. Others believe teachers should simply do what they're told.[23]

In the innovation schools teachers can begin with what interests students and with what fits their aptitudes.

---

23. Early in my time with these questions I spoke to the summer meeting of the Minnesota School Boards Association. In setting out the case for site-management I mentioned the schools in Florida where students began turning down the lights and the air conditioning, knowing the savings could be used for school activities. I had been sitting next to Joan Parent, a long-time board member, former president of the Minnesota and of the National School Boards Association. When I finished she turned to me. She didn't say "Nice talk" or "Thanks for coming". She just made reference to that story. "I'd never have handled it like that. I'd have sent them a directive to turn off the lights and turn off the air conditioning, and if they didn't do it I'd fire them". And she turned and walked away.

Some of the schools that have appeared in the chartered sector do this. Project-based learning also enhances motivation. These schools, their 'advisers', begin by asking: "What's your passion?" They then help the student shape a program of learning around those interests.

One day I heard a student at Minnesota New Country School telling a staff person from the Education Commission of the States he was trying to understand why people in Kansas were getting elected-to and unelected-from the state board of education. This was requiring him to understand the debate about evolution.

An adviser could make a nice project out of that. Learn something about genetics. Read Darwin's *Voyage of the Beagle* and *Origin of Species*. Understand the theological controversy these books produced in England in the late 19th century. Read Inherit the Wind about the Scopes trial in Tennessee. Pretty soon the project has pulled together science, religion, drama, literature, history and political science.

Remarkable things sometimes happen when young people can study what interests them. Often under traditional arrangements they have to do these things outside regular school hours—Bill Gates was programming at night while in eighth grade—or outside the school. Google for 'student competitions': See how much effort young people expend to learn what school does not teach; think about the level at which you see them performing.

Asking what interests students opens a larger question about how we define achievement; about what we mean by 'student performance' and about what success is for a school.

Let's move to that next.

CHAPTER 6

Use a broader concept of 'achievement'

Schools in the innovation sector will broaden
both the range of subjects studied and the notion of student
performance. Today's constricted concept of 'achievement' works
to narrow what's studied. Higher achievement probably depends
on broadening the concept of 'learning'.

In the standard-enlightened notion of 'school reform' the concept of achievement is pretty much limited to knowledge and skills in English and math. A school is deemed 'high-performing' if it produces students who score high on the state assessments in these academic areas.

Proficiency in English and math surely is important. It forms a base for the learning to come later. But it is obvious there is more to academic achievement than English and math, and more to achievement than academics. Cognitive skills are important but so are the non-cognitive skills. And though proficiency is important, so is excellence. With a broader definition of achievement America will see and will get more achievement.

The need for this ought to be obvious. *Is there any other area of life that uses a one-dimensional notion of success and of quality?* Think about your job, your city, your employer, your neighborhood, your house, your school, your church; the restaurant you patronize and the doctor you go to. Or, for that matter, the people you know; your family, even. There are positives and negatives about each, are there not? Think about your car: There is initial cost and operating cost. There is fuel economy; there are speed and style, capacity and safety. Probably you weigh and balance all those considerations. *'Quality' is everywhere multi-dimensional, is it not?* And judgments are made on-balance.

Field of Achievement

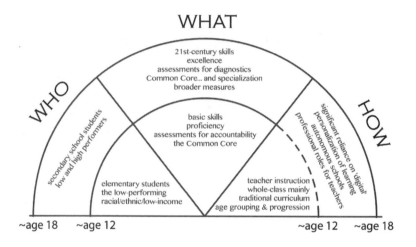

Nor does the judgment need always to be quantitative. For most of us, judgments about our lawyer, our doctor, our church, our job *are* non-quantifiable; are based essentially on satisfaction. John Goodlad argued for satisfaction as a measure of success in *Educational Renewal.*[24]

The move by the innovation schools to test broader and more sophisticated dimensions of achievement and of 'performance' will help the difficult policy discussion about achievement in several ways.

In these 'different' schools it will:

---

24. *Tomorrow's Schools*, Chapter 7, page 209.

... highlight non-academic skills and knowledge.

The so-called non-cognitive skills are important, in themselves and because they assist in developing the academic knowledge and skills.

Professor James Heckman at the University of Chicago has written and spoken extensively about this. Paul Tough's *How Children Succeed* relies heavily on Heckman's work. So have others, going back many years. Ken Kay created and for about a decade led the Partnership for 21st Century Skills (now housed with the Council of Chief State School Officers). In 1987 in her presidential address to the American Educational Research Association Lauren Resnick talked about the differences between "Learning In School and Out".[25] Whitehead, in *The Aims of Education*, counseled against "inert ideas": Education, he said, "is the acquisition of the art of the utilisation of knowledge".

Traditionalists resist; disparaging non-academic skills as 'soft'; arguing they can't be defined and can't be measured, so needn't be considered. There is a high level of resistance to 'satisfaction' as a legitimate basis for parents' judgment about their child's school—yielding, grudgingly, only where the question turns on the child's physical safety.

Business appears confused. Those speaking for businesses and business associations in the policy debate tend to defend the one-dimensional notion of achievement. Closer to the point of hiring and in the human resources departments, business people seem to look beyond the transcript. Listen to Lowell Hellervik,

---

25. Resnick is a professor of education at the University of Pittsburgh. "Briefly", she said in her address, "schooling focuses on the individual's performance, whereas out-of-school mental work is often socially shared. Schooling aims to foster unaided thought, whereas mental work outside school usually involves cognitive tools. School cultivates symbolic thinking, whereas mental activity outside school engages directly with objects and situations. Finally, schooling aims to teach general skills and knowledge, whereas situation-specific competencies dominate outside."

whose organization of selection psychologists, Personnel Decisions, Inc., created a pre-employment test now given millions of times in a variety of industries and organizations for a variety of jobs:

"Clearly, cognitive skills are important for success both in schools and outside school. However, anyone who claims that cognitive knowledge is the only thing that matters flies in the face of hiring authorities' personal experience as well as the scientific data. . . . Employers and many academics who studied the test found it to be a significant predictor of success for people in many jobs; a predictor of "conscientiousness". Conscientiousness is highly prized by organizations; is a personal characteristic that does not require traditional cognitive skills. It can be taught, since its components are behavioral, such as getting to work on time."

. . . call attention to the variation in aptitudes.

You do not hear much about aptitudes in the education policy discussion. This is curious because aptitudes are real and are important for learning. Psychologists have found that different individuals really are good at different things. There is more than one way of being smart; more than one way of learning, as Howard Gardner demonstrated in his work on "multiple intelligences".[26]

Work with psychologists at the University of Minnesota led to the creation of the Ball Aptitude Battery. This assessment can distinguish aptitudes that are verbal/conceptual/abstract from those that are spatial/visual/tactile. I remember John Goodlad talking to the alumni of the University of Minnesota College of Education about his two sons. One, he said, could understand a

---

26. An interesting question arises: Is a student failing if not doing well in a field for which s/he has no aptitude? Should performance be judged relative to aptitude?

clock if you explained how a clock worked. The other understood a clock only when he took it apart to see how it worked.

... stress personalized, competency-based, learning.

Students arrive at school with different levels of knowledge and of attainment. Some come to kindergarten knowing how to read and having large vocabularies. Others cannot read and have limited (English) vocabularies. So personalization is important for achievement.

It seems obvious, too, that getting students moving at different speeds would improve achievement. Those needing more time would get more time and those able to go faster would go faster. Learning would improve on both counts.

Traditional school, whole-group-instruction combined with age-based progression, fails on both counts; boring some students while leaving others behind—to the point where some are classified as learning-disabled and put into special education.

Conventional school is like a bus rolling down the highway; going too rapidly for some and too slowly for others, providing no opportunity for a student to get off to explore something interesting s/he sees along the way. In the discussion about education policy age-grading is assumed; almost never questioned. People ask a child, "What grade are you in?" Educators ask, "Is she *at grade-level*?"

Educators who use the approach (ungracefully) termed Response to Intervention (RtI) start where each child is; check continually to see whether each is on track to proficiency in reading by third grade; correcting course if a child is not. They describe the traditional approach as, "Wait, to Fail".[27] The approach was largely developed in Minnesota and has spread

---

27. RtI might better be termed 'Intervene, to Succeed'. Learning disability, it turns out, might be a characteristic more of the instruction than of the child.

nationally. It reduces failure and cuts placements into special education. It works also with regular students. Kim Gibbons, who heads the St. Croix River Education District in Minnesota, says people sometimes describe the successful children as 'gifted'. "They're not gifted", she says. "They just learned to read early."

Current efforts to improve standards and assessment accept age-grading. At the Atlanta meeting of the Education Commission of the States in 2012 I asked Mike Cohen, head of Achieve, why he had been discussing the Common Core entirely in terms of grade-levels. Mike said: "It's an age-graded system. We take the system as we find it". Earlier I'd heard the same thing from Henry Hipps of Microsoft when he was talking about the Shared Learning Collaborative.

Personalizing learning makes it possible to break with age-grading and move to competency-based progression. Why not? A high school tennis coach can move a seventh-grader onto the varsity based on the student's ability to win matches. Why can't students 'play on the varsity', similarly, in math?

Again, the split screen strategy would not force all schools away from age-grading or from any other given. The idea is to let some schools move to competency-based progression if they wish; then let that approach spread if and as it proves effective.

To a degree, of course, achievement *is* beginning to be competency-based; as, with the post-secondary option Minnesota introduced in 1985. It can be expanded significantly.

. . . encourage specialization in high school.

The happy group of little children commonly seen illustrating books, magazine articles and television programs about school reveals the preoccupation with elementary school in the current discussion. It is more than wanting not to show surly teen-agers:

Conventional school reform truly is almost entirely about proficiency in the early grades.[28]

It is a mistake not to talk about achievement for older students. At about age 13 student engagement fades and achievement tails off. High school *is* a problem.

In the innovating schools it would be reasonable to let secondary students follow their own interests; to let them specialize in what interests them and in what they do well. Not all students will be interested in, or will be good at, all subjects. But specialization is not wrong. The country needs excellence. Surely it is obvious that excellence requires specialization.

... help students succeed in what they want to do next

The push for 'standards' seems to have accepted without question that standards would be *exit* standards. It was as if school were a walled city with gates on all sides and someone decided that all those leaving needed to be identically dressed and provisioned whatever their destination. Why did policy not think instead in terms of *entrance* standards related to the different destinations toward which different students were heading?

All around high school the institutions young people want to get into next—the building trades, college, the military, business, government, the nonprofit world—have standards for admission. Often these are high standards. What if we were to show young people early in their high-school years what specifically they need to know and be able to do *in order to be accepted where they want to go next*? Might that clarify their personal

---

28. At a national meeting in 2013, after a presentation about how to produce 'high-performing' schools, someone asked: "How much of this is about high school?" The panelists looked at each other. After a while one said, "Better feeder schools will mean better high schools". Another said basically: High schools are a pit. That was all.

goals? Might that enhance their motivation and improve their achievement; help get them "college-and career-ready"?

Isn't it obvious that standards should be those needed for a particular post-secondary education and for a particular vocational career? A math standard set for everyone would be far too low for a student wanting to go into a science or math career, would it not?

. . . improve equity in the system.

A broader definition of achievement will highlight the way today's narrow definition of achievement creates a problem of equity.

The one-dimensional notion—good scores on English and math—basically says children are succeeding if they can do what the children of middle-class parents can do; if they have aptitudes are verbal/abstract/conceptual. Other kinds of achievement are not credited. Bob Wedl, Minnesota's former commissioner of education, suggests this diminishes the achievement of racial and ethic minorities: If we were to define achievement as the ability to speak two or more languages, he asks, which students would be 'high-achieving'?[29]

The Ball Foundation found that school people, whose aptitudes tend to be verbal/ abstract/conceptual, sometimes define those aptitudes as 'smart'; so regard students whose aptitudes are spatial, visual and tactile as 'not smart' and have sometimes counseled the latter into careers for which they were not suited and thus into lives that were frustrating and unsuccessful.

Jack Frymier thought it was quite unfair for adults not themselves at risk to be imposing failure on young people just getting started in life. Governor Perpich, when pressed by the

---

29. A middle-school principal told Wedl about a young East African child who on a visit to the Minneapolis Institute of Arts excitedly ran over to one of the exhibits and read his classmates what was written there. It was written, of course, in Arabic.

business leadership to buy into the conventional methods of assessing 'success', declined to do so. "I've seen too many people who passed tests and failed life", he told associates, "and too many people who failed tests and passed life".

... ease the politics of 'the achievement gap' debate.

Today's discussion about 'the achievement gap' is difficult because it defines achievement as the difference in median scores (on the assessments of English and math) between racial, ethnic and income groups. The idea of closing the gap, it appears, is to make the median scores identical for all groups.

But how exactly is the gap to *close*? Most of the discussion is about bringing up the students now-low-performing. And there are ways to do that. But raising their scores does not close the gap if the higher-performing students improve at the same time. No one suggests the high-performing should not or will not also improve. So how then does the gap close? No one says.

Surely, too, the differences in median proficiency scores is the hardest gap to close. Why not start instead by closing the gap between current-attainment and proficient? Today the proportion of students meeting the standards in English and math is lower in some groups than in others. Why not concentrate first on getting all students to proficient; worry later about some being farther above proficient than others?

The politics of the discussion would ease were we to see that 'the gap' is a function of the way we define 'achievement'. Broaden the definition, and—per Bob Wedl's comment about multiple languages—the concept of the gap changes. Broaden the concept of achievement and we might see most all students achieving.

A former governor recently spoke disapprovingly of "setting the bar at a different height for each student". Yet perhaps standards *should* be set relative to the individual student's potential.

A teen-age boy should be able to jump chest-height. But many can jump higher; and do, in the competition of a track meet. The bar keeps being raised for the best. This seems not inequitable or unfair.

It is important to be realistic. If we define successful performance as all students clearing the same height, that height is bound to be low—which will not get the country the learning it needs. Set the bar high for everyone and the failure rate for students and schools will be high—which is not tolerable politically. The practical way out of this dilemma is to have a broader concept of achievement, and different standards for the different goals of different students.

The high jump is not the only event in a track meet. One senior at a high school near Saint Paul probably would not do well in the high jump. But she ranks top in America in the shot-put and discus. Is she not succeeding? If we respect accomplishments in a broader range of fields, academic and non-academic, we will see more, perhaps most, young people being successful at something. Why would we not do that?

In the innovation sector assessment and accountability also change

It is hard to think of anything that suppresses innovation more than the one-dimensional concept of achievement. So it is essential that the schools in the innovation sector be able themselves to define what they intend to achieve—for which, of course, they will be accountable. They will probably want their students to learn to read and compute. They will probably want to include dimensions of achievement beyond that. The judgment about their success will be made on-balance.

Some chartered schools operate on this principle. These schools feel strongly enough about their students coming out with broader knowledge and additional skills that they are willing to risk lower scores on the conventional assessments, confident their students will do well enough to get by. That comes at some cost to their reputation and to their continued existence, given the growing orthodoxy about 'quality'.

The advocates of 'quality charters' are working now to get state laws amended to make student achievement, *narrowly defined,* the sole basis on which a charter can be renewed. This serves their goal; helps build a rationale they believe will enable the chartered sector to grow and gradually to displace the urban district schools.

But, for all the reasons laid out above, so narrow a concept of achievement might not well serve the public interest. It is possible that other and broader definitions of achievement might better serve both students and the nation's interest. We will never know until we let people try things . . . until we free up schools and teachers to test these possibilities while, again, in mainline schools the conventional model continues to operate.

The split-screen strategy is a hedging of risk. It lets the country be trying both improvement and innovation at the same time so we can see which of the two—or whether a combination of the two—will prove the better approach, over time.

CHAPTER 7

Treat teen-agers increasingly as adults

We could improve the achievement of teen-agers if we would modify the old institution of adolescence—that 'artificial extension of childhood' that holds young people back from doing all they can do. In their interest and in the country's interest we should challenge them harder and ask them to take more responsibility for their learning.

Why does the whole effort to improve learning go on with no one questioning the institution of adolescence that works so powerfully against it?

In years of listening to the education policy discussion I had never heard adolescence mentioned until Sheldon White, then professor of psychology at Harvard, put it in perspective at the gathering held for Ted Sizer when he left Brown University in May 1999. "A separate society for the young, prolonging childhood" was how White described it; created a century ago by a coming-together of the child-welfare movement, the laws against child labor, the new high schools and the special legislation for juvenile offenders.

Earlier in America, and in many parts of the world still, you were adult at puberty. Up to 1905 about 40 per cent of American 16-year-olds were in school and about 40 per cent in work. Some of that work was exploitive and dangerous, in mines and factories. Soon that began to change, and after 1930 young people moved rapidly out of work.

To absorb those millions of teen-agers America vastly expanded high school. Today about 90 per cent of 16-year-olds are in school. And a popular notion now is to keep students in school even longer. In 2013 Minnesota's Legislature extended the legal leaving-age from 16 to 17.

Like most reforms this one was filled with good intentions. But its effect has been to discriminate against those young people whose experience, aptitudes or inclination does not fit them for academic work. It also blocks those whose abilities and experiences enable them to achieve more, sooner.

"Adults have disappeared from the lives of adolescents," Deborah Meier, founder of the Central Park East School in New York City, said that day at Brown. "We have deliberately created [schools] in which it is impossible for adults to know kids well. Young people know no one but their peers. And all this gets worse the closer they get to adulthood."

The motives for the creation of the institution did not entirely put the interest of children first. Organized labor, then growing in influence, wanted young people out of the labor force. And as White noted, adolescence created millions of jobs for adult professionals: people in corrections, in social work—and in schools. The education system is itself deeply vested in the institution of adolescence.

A century after it appeared, the institution of adolescence is itself a given. Few today can remember when 'work' was a major route upward. Today the world of work is closed until one has the credentials. 'School' is now the route by which young people prepare for their career; get their credentials. In school vocational training has been eclipsed by academic study.[30]

---

30. Pasi Sahlberg—from Finland, now visiting at the Harvard Graduate School of Education—asks a relevant question: How can students be 'career-ready' if school has not provided them work experience during their school years?

Young people still do work, as someone pointed out at the Sizer gathering. But not so they can advance: They work so they can earn money for college and so they can be marketed-to as consumers.

Some years later I came across a Commentary in Education Week titled "Let's Abolish High School". It was written by a student of White's, Robert Epstein, by then a professor at the University of California at San Diego. Epstein quickly disclaimed a serious intention to do away with high school: He was trying, he wrote, to get people to think about the damage the institution of adolescence does to young people and to our society. He is serious about that, as he explains fully in *The Case Against Adolescence* (now re-titled *Teen 2.0*).

Epstein does not disagree about the moronic behavior of many teens. But he says adolescence 'infantilizes' young people. Deny them serious responsibilities, keep them out of real work, give them virtually no contact with adults, tell them they have no function except to be schooled (and marketed-to): Why wouldn't they behave as they do?

I drew on his analysis in 2008 when asked to review *The Dumbest Generation* by Mark Bauerlein, a professor of English at Emory University. The book is an assault on people under 30, obsessed with their digital devices, disinclined to read and almost unable to write.

I quoted what Paul Johnson, a British popular historian, wrote in *The Birth of the Modern* about the accomplishments in the years after 1815 by young people who came from truly disadvantaged backgrounds, who had almost no schooling and who went to work early.

It was a time when new fields of activity provided opportunities for young people to get serious responsibilities early and to rise as rapidly as their abilities and energies would take them. They did amazing things. Some of their roads, bridges and other public works still stand in England, still in use.

» *Michael Faraday, the scientist, "was born poor, the son of a Yorkshire blacksmith. He had no education other than a few years at a school for the poor, but as a bookbinder's apprentice he read the works he bound . . ."*

» *John Otley, the geologist, "had no education apart from village schooling and set up as a basket-maker."*

» *James Naysmith, the engineer, "started as an apprentice coach painter. His son, James, inventor of the steam hammer, made a brass cannon at the age of nine."*

» *Henry Maudsley, 'perhaps the greatest of all the machine-tool inventors, began work at 12 as a powder-monkey in a cartridge works."*

» *Matthew Murray, "the great engine designer, began as a kitchen boy and butler. Richard Roberts, brilliant inventor of power looms, was a shoemaker's son, had virtually no education and began as a quarry laborer. John Kennedy, the first great builder of iron ships, was another poor Scot who received no schooling except in summer and started as a carpenter's boy."*

In *Longitude* Dava Sobel tells the story of John Harrison who solved "the greatest scientific problem of his time". With no formal education and no apprenticeship to any watchmaker he invented a clock that would carry the true time from the home port to any point in the world, enabling mariners at last to know their east/west location.

In *The Maritime History of Massachusetts* Samuel Eliot Morison writes about Mary Patten, wife of the captain of a clipper ship. "In 1858 on a voyage around Cape Horn, her husband fell ill. The first mate was in irons for insubordination; the second mate was ignorant of navigation. Mrs. Patten had made herself mistress of the art of navigation during a previous voyage. She took command, and for 52 days she navigated the ship of 1800 tons, tending her husband the while, and took both safely into San Francisco". She was 19.

Wartime generates many such stories. In *With Wings Like Eagles: A History of the Battle of Britain* Michael Korda writes that by late-summer 1940 more and more of those flying the Spitfires and Hurricanes were in our terms high school seniors. Nineteen-year-old women were ferrying the planes from the factories to the aerodromes. In Russia Nadia Popova started flying at 16 and at 18 in flimsy plywood aircraft flew hundreds of missions bombing German encampments at night. At 18 Cecil Phillips in America and Mavis Lever in England had begun breaking codes.

I ended the review by asking:

Are we to believe that these abilities have been lost, in young people today? Or is our society simply failing to let young people have, early, the responsibilities and opportunities needed for them to achieve?

Adolescence simultaneously relieved young people of responsibilities and brought prohibitions that denied them opportunities. If you're not an adult you can't do adult things: be employed full-time, inherit property, vote, seek or refuse medical treatment, sign contracts, file lawsuits, marry without parental consent. One insurance company still pushes to raise the legal driving age to 18.

After 1950 its effects were compounded by the cultural shift that public-opinion analyst Daniel Yankelovich details in *New Rules*—from the ethic of self-denial to the ethic of self-fulfillment. So many people had so much money it was impossible to say no to cars, clothes, guitars, computers, travel. No wonder youth behavior changed dramatically. With prosperity a new youth culture appeared: music, dress, drugs, sex.

Adults, disliking this teen-age behavior, tried to control it, tightening the restrictions. Which of course bred resentment, stimulating more challenging behavior. Which generated still more restrictions. Curfews. Can't drive. Can't drink. "No entry except with adult". Blocked access to the internet. Sex under 18 criminalized. No cigarettes. Dress codes. "Parental Consent Required". And in school metal detectors, video surveillance, armed guards, no hoods and "No Cell Phones!".

The restrictions created by adolescence have made young people arguably the most discriminated-against class of people in our society. And nobody sees it. Good people who would never utter a racial or ethnic slur think nothing of referring to young adults as 'kids'.

Though told education is the only way up, most young people find the schooling they are offered neither motivating nor relevant; affording them little say in what they study, in how and how rapidly they learn or in the way their school runs. Yet few things about the education policy discussion are more stunning than the absence of the student voice. You go to meeting after meeting and seldom if ever hear a student consulted. It is almost entirely an adult discussion.

Why, for heaven's sake? Who knows more about school and learning? How many businesses would not want to know what users thought of their service?

Perhaps adults in the K-12 system fear what students might say. When Elinor Burkett, after Columbine, was looking to spend a year in a suburban high school principals told her, in effect: "You have to be crazy to think I'd let you see what goes on in my school". Read *Another Planet*: Think how different it is from the discussions about high school in the education policy books.

But—uncomfortable as it might prove—why *not* seek the advice of those who know most about what goes on in school? Why does K-12 remain a system that will not listen to its customers?

Most important: What if those talents *are* still there in young people; suppressed by the institution of adolescence?

How might we release that reservoir of talent?

It will take years to take down the institution of adolescence—as it has taken years to change other old social institutions. The way to begin, though, is to create some schools that let young people learn as fast and go as far in every field as their efforts and abilities will take them.

Schools in the innovation sector would introduce competency-based progression—as per Chapter 6. They would move more young people into essentially adult roles earlier in life, as John Goodlad and others have proposed. They could open new opportunities for work, crediting and respecting what young people learn outside school—as employers often do.

Here are two examples from just one community college near where I live.

In 2009 while finishing eighth grade (at 13) Caleb Kumar earned an associate of arts degree from North Hennepin Community College. At 15 he received a $25,000 scholarship from the Davidson Institute for Talent Development for developing an algorithm to automate the diagnosis of bladder cancer.

In 1998 Rob and Ryan Weber, twins, got an AA degree from North Hennepin through Minnesota's post-secondary enrollment option just before graduating from Osseo Senior High. They'd already been starting computer software businesses. Today NativeX, a firm they started in 2000 with older brother Aaron, has over 160 employees and offices in Sartell Minnesota, Minneapolis and San Francisco.

You might have seen the film about Laura Dekker. She was sailing single-handed in Holland at six. At 13 she decided to sail alone around the world. The authorities had a fit (about her leaving school) but her parents agreed. At 14 she set off in a 38-foot ketch, stopped along the way and returned safely at 16.

America could get far more from its young people if it did adapt school to let them move faster. When you Google for 'youth accomplishment' you'll see that outside school young people today are doing things we usually associate with adults. But this is mostly in fields adults can't master or don't want to enter: sports, entertainment, digital electronics. The routines of school, the institution of adolescence, block off young people from opportunities to do more, sooner, in mainline fields.

Accelerating learning, moving students on to post-secondary at 16, is positive for the economics of education as well. Minnesota, for example, has about 75,000 juniors and 75,000 seniors; spends about $10,000 on each. Multiply $10,000 by 150,000 and you get a rather large number. And that's *per year*. And Minnesota is less than 2 per cent of the nation.

Mainline school is unlikely to take the lead in this—which argues for involving the organizations that work with youth outside of school. We could enlarge the role of the non-school learning organizations: the science museums and art galleries and zoos and organizations like 4-H. These are careful about suggesting they 'educate': They worry the K-12 institution, better financed and possessive about its claim on learning, would block them out or try to take them over. But there is potential here.

An effort to innovate with school would not directly reach the institution of adolescence, which lies outside it; surrounds it; influences it. A real attack on this problem lies outside the area of education policy. But if someone, somewhere—in journalism, in politics; in one of the foundations—were to make this a cause, were to suggest that young people are the last major untapped reservoir of talent in our economy . . . things might change.

We could start by picking up Epstein's idea to make adultness competency-based rather than age-based. He does not suggest abolishing 'adolescence'. He proposes that young people be allowed to test out of its restrictions—as he says many could. He has developed an assessment of 'adultness'—of responsibility and maturity—given thousands of times. Between the ages of 15 and 85, Epstein finds, the proportion of persons demonstrating those qualities is essentially independent of age.

Some schools we see in the chartered sector do this. Avalon School in Saint Paul, for example, has a constitution that delegates to students significant authority over dress and conduct. The school finds that the students make and enforce stricter rules than its adults could make and enforce.

Trusting teens, treating them more like adults, is an idea unlikely to be adopted quickly. But it would be worth trying: People often do live up to what's expected of them.

Again: Competency-based progression implies personalized learning. And the tradition of K-12 education is, instead, "batch processing". So a key change—an innovation, if you will—is precisely to personalize learning.

Let's think next about how to do that.

CHAPTER 8

Let more schools personalize learning

*The digital electronics now revolutionizing the handling of information are bound to transform school and learning. Initially the response is to 'blend' digital into traditional school. To realize its full potential there will need to be schools able to put 'digital' to **non**-traditional use, personalizing learning.*

Lewis Perelman was ahead of his time in 1992 when he wrote about 'hyperlearning' in *School's Out*. Re-forming, incrementally improving, school is a waste of time, he thought. Standards will become ceilings rather than floors. The right ideas for learning are more, better, faster, cheaper. Learning is going to bypass school.

In 1992 the implications of digital electronics were not so clear. The World Wide Web had been created only in 1991. The effort to introduce 'standards' was becoming the strategy of choice. 'Standards' was compatible with traditional school. 'Hyperlearning', too radical, was not admitted to the policy discussion.

Today it's clearer that a revolution *is* coming in the way people learn. To cite John Lienhard again: Every significant change in the handling of information produces a fundamental change in education.

At the end of a talk in Minneapolis about Google disrupting 'old media'—newspapers, books, magazines, music publishing, advertising, the Postal Service—Ken Auletta was asked: Is 'school' old media? Of course, he said.

Today 'digital' is rushing in. The education publications are filled with ads for new instructional software, for teacher professional development, for new hardware, for interconnection. Books pour out describing the wonders ahead. Parents support it. And many of the students are good at it; start early; are skilled with the electronics. Their capacity is a big asset.

How is the new technology to be used? Will it be for the teacher or for the students? Will it enhance the standardization of classroom teaching or will it individualize learning? Will it reinforce or disrupt traditional school?

There are bound to be strong pressures not to let it disrupt conventional school. People will likely try to fit the electronics into the existing way of doing things—as happens in most fields when new devices appear. 'Movie cameras' when they first appeared were sometimes used to film stage plays.[31]

It will be tempting to fit 'digital' into the age-grading of traditional school and into the technology of teacher instruction. That might not be good education, but it does let the districts introduce a single digital program in all schools.

To some degree this results from the vendor pressure that introduced regulations in the early days. One Minnesota superintendent attributes that to the textbook publishers. "I can put anything I want into a classroom if it's print on paper. If it's print on screen I have to get permission from the state department".

---

31. I remember wandering once into an empty math classroom in Humboldt High School in Saint Paul. On each student desk was a computer terminal. From each a wire led up to the teacher's desk. At her console the teacher could watch all the students' work. I thought: It was like this in my elementary school—except that the teacher walked the aisles, looking down at the students' papers. Today the teacher doesn't get the exercise.

It seems hard to imagine *state* adoption of learning software, comparable to state adoption of textbooks. Yet there are reasons for the digital industry to press for large-scale adoption, to minimize their cost of sales. It could be a challenge to get big companies to want to sell school by school, classroom by classroom.

Perhaps what happens will depend on the way K-12 is structured to make decisions: by district or by school.

Recently the point of decision about digital has been drifting upward. The marketing is less now to teachers than it was a few years ago. "Who is your customer?" I asked a vendor showing his science program at an iNACOL meeting in Minneapolis. "The schools", he said. "Literally? I asked: "The principal and teachers?" "Of course not", he said. "The district".

But the implication of the electronics is to return decisions to the classroom. Fundamentally digital electronics bring together the capacity to personalize with the need to personalize. Students arrive with widely varying levels of attainment in vocabulary, in reading, in math. With their potential to adapt to these differences the electronics open the way to a new technology of learning. So the key is the teachers; the school.

Albert Shanker could see this early. Visiting Saint Paul's new Saturn School of Tomorrow in 1982 he said:

> *Our country is unwilling to sort and stream students the way some European nations do. So the American teacher is confronted by a mixed-ability classroom. This creates a hopeless dilemma: Teach to the students doing best and soon there are behavior problems in the classroom. Teach to the neediest students and soon some parents are calling saying their child isn't being challenged. The answer is to individualize. But we can't provide a teacher for every student. Technology is the way out.*

This whole discussion might be clearer if we redefine 'technology'.

'Labor, capital and technology'

When they hear 'technology' most people think about things visible in today's offices and factories: tools and machinery; robots. In the world of digital they think of the computers, the digital devices, perhaps of the endless stacks of blinking servers in a data center. And, of course, of the software.

But this use of the term confuses 'technology' with what the economists call 'capital', one of the factors of production along with labor. Some economists more helpfully distinguish between 'capital' and 'technology', defining technology as *the way capital and labor are combined*. The factors of production then become labor, capital and technology.

The classic example is the assembly line. Before Henry Ford changed things a worker or a few workers built a whole automobile. In Ford's factory each worker did one thing over and over as the cars came down the line. The new technology was not the machinery on the line: It was the different way of organizing work, the different way of combining capital and labor.

It's interesting to apply this non-traditional definition to school:

» The technology of traditional school has been whole-class teacher instruction. It was not capital-intensive: mostly books, the blackboard, the movie projector or TV set. It was *labor*-intensive: a teacher for every 25 students. The teacher was the worker; the students passive. It was expensive even with teachers not highly paid. Most recently school has been heavying-up the capital—as by giving the teacher an electronic blackboard. But that does not change the technology: It essentially mechanizes the technology of teacher-instruction.[32]

---

32. A favorite photo, taken from the back of a classroom, shows every student with a portable computer—and the same picture on every screen.

» Alternatively it is possible to arrange for the digital electronics to change the way capital and labor are combined; creating a new technology of personalized student learning. This changes the 'labor' as well. The teacher is no longer the only worker. The students now do more of the work; learning individually and helping other students (peer-teaching).[33] Teachers' work upgrades to planning, advising and evaluating.

A fascinating case of changing-the-technology appeared in Minnesota about 2008 in a district near Saint Paul when a teacher undertook to personalize his third-grade classroom. He grew up in south India; came to America to study graphics. Halfway through a career in the printing industry he decided to become a teacher.

On the job he quickly found that what he had been trained to do and told to do was not effective. The September assessments showed the level of attainment among his students ranging from the 10th percentile and below to the 90th percentile and above. He concluded he had to individualize.

He asked if he could cash-out the value of the whiteboard the district proposed to give him. The administrators said no. So with his own and his wife's money, plus some contributed dollars, he bought PCs, voice recorders and printed materials. He selected gaming software for the students to learn English and math. His classroom was transformed. Students are active, moving, talking to each other; totally engaged. He had changed the technology from whole-class instruction to personalized learning.[34]

---

33. A meta-analysis at Stanford University in the early 1980s, comparing four interventions—longer day and year, smaller classes, computerization and peer-teaching—found that peer teaching was the most effective (cost not considered). Yet peer teaching almost never appears in the policy discussion about improving learning.

34. To see this classroom go to http://www.educationevolving.org/pai.

It was an important test of personalization. But few teachers can invest that kind of private money to personalize their classroom. So how can we enable more teachers to replicate that change in the technology of learning?

Create incentives—reasons + opportunities— for the teachers

Some teachers will quickly see the need and the potential. But old ways die hard; the old technology of whole-group instruction will be slow to change. How to make the change move faster?

Certainly it will help if we let the change benefit the workers; the teachers. Incentives matter.

To accomplish this, arrange things on the innovation side of the split screen for schools to put teachers in the situation of American farmers after 1870. The family farm took up new machinery and new methods rapidly. Why? Because—as Norman Macrae, then its deputy editor, wrote in the Economist in 1984 after talking with Max Geldens of McKinsey—in the family-farm arrangement in the American Midwest and Great Plains work and ownership were combined. New equipment and new practices made the farmers' work easier and their investment more rewarding. Farmers became hugely better off. Agriculture became vastly more productive.

In manufacturing, by contrast, where work and ownership were separated, the rewards from new equipment went to the factory owners who employed the workers. Initially some workers tried to block the introduction of new machines and new methods. When that failed they accepted the reality of change and organized to fight for a share of the productivity gains. This industrial conflict is still with us—conspicuously, in the 'factory model' of conventional K-12.

Test this workers-as-owners idea yourself. Ask your friends which of the two prior stages of the economy—the agricultural era or the industrial era—the new information era is most like. See if most don't answer: like agriculture. Then ask: Why then do we have education organized on the factory model? Why *don't* we arrange to have education arranged, like farming, to give the teachers incentives—reasons and opportunities—to take up new methods in their own interest?

That is hardly conventional policy today. Pressures from various directions will try to keep digital from disrupting traditional school. Some perhaps feel that 'blending' digital into the traditional technology of teacher-instruction makes it seem less threatening. Some might hope that fitting the new electronics into traditional school will ease the concern that commercial interests will exploit their lower costs and make 'excessive profits'. Some might feel that downplaying 'online' and 'virtual' comports with the public perception of 'real school'; an adult with 25 students all attentive to the teacher talking.[35]

The districts' impulse to control teachers' work, their reluctance to allow teachers discretion over curriculum and pedagogy, extends beyond the use of the digital electronics. It can be found in the way some are now scripting teachers' lessons within the traditional technology of whole-class teacher-instruction. Districts do feel the pressures to standardize and to lock down on what data show 'works'.

For all these reasons the practical strategy will—again – need to explore the disruptive potential of the new technology *in a separate* set *of innovation schools* organized to give teachers real authority to adapt to the students; to try things.

How to create this condition—in which the teachers carry more of the authority over the learning—becomes the next question we need to consider.

---

35. "A good teacher quiets the classroom", Bill Gates said, more than once, at the National Forum of the Education Commission of the States in Atlanta in 2012.

CHAPTER 9

Give more teachers professional roles

Conventional 'reform' sees itself improving teachers'
effectiveness. Yet by diminishing their role it might have the
opposite effect. As learning personalizes, teachers' role needs to
enlarge. If teachers can control what matters for student success
teachers will accept accountability for student success.

Schools on the innovation side of the split screen will treat teachers as professionals—in the sense of trusting them to know how the job should be done. The personalization of learning makes this essential because in the school it is only the teachers who know the students as individuals.

It will be entirely possible . . . will make basic sense . . . to let these teachers operate through partnerships of the sort we know in other white-collar vocations we call professional. As professional partners they will make the decisions about how the school runs, doing the administration themselves or having the administrators working for them.

This is not hypothetical. Schools organized as professional partnerships (sometimes formally as workers' cooperatives) began to appear in Minnesota's chartered sector about 1993. In about 2000 the model spread successfully into the big-city environment in Milwaukee. In one form or another partnerships have since been appearing in other states.

The idea of delegating decisions to the school and of vesting this authority with teachers organized collegially does not work in theory. The received theory is that a school must have 'a strong leader'. "Somebody *has* to be in charge", people say. Also, K-12 holds to a single-leader model, assuming, hoping . . . pretending, perhaps . . . that one person can be at the same time the best teacher and the best administrator.

The professional-partnership arrangement changes all that. The authority pyramid inverts, and school moves to the dual-leader model typical of partnerships in most areas. (Think of the managing partner and the administrator of a law firm, or the chief of the medical staff and the executive of a hospital.)

Teaching has never been a true profession. It does not require a graduate professional education. It does not pay a professional salary. It does not confer full professional status: Teachers do not get the trust accorded electricians or plumbers to know how the job should be done.

But there are now encouraging efforts to invent and develop new ways of organizing teaching and learning; models in which teachers do make the key decisions about learning. And in the schools now taking this approach it does seem to be working— as, of course, it works in law and medicine and in accounting, consulting, architecture, engineering and auditing.

When something moves from one field to another a kind of innovation occurs. John Lienhard notes in *How Invention Begins* that the steam engine had been used for years to pump water out of mines before someone thought to use it to drive a boat or pull a train. In this sense transferring the partnership idea into K-12 is an innovation. It can help turn K-12 into a self-improving system—and on the policy and political front can help with the contentious discussion currently about teacher effectiveness and teacher accountability.

Persons in the software field use this photo in presentations all over the country to help people understand that to visualize personalized learning it's essential to step outside the concept of 'the class'. This is Minnesota New Country School, at Henderson MN; a grade 7-12 secondary that uses project-based learning and is run by a cooperative of teachers.

TRUSTING TEACHERS WITH SCHOOL SUCCESS

"Lively"
—Deborah Meier

"A must-read!"
—John Merrow

WHAT HAPPENS WHEN TEACHERS CALL THE SHOTS

KIM FARRIS-BERG AND EDWARD DIRKSWAGER
WITH AMY JUNGE

For *Trusting Teachers* the authors examined about a dozen schools in which teachers "call the shots". Its findings provide the basis for the effort Education|Evolving is making to build awareness of the benefits of this model . . . and to explain what teachers change when, collegially, as professionals, they carry the authority and the accountability for student and school success.

For a copy, go to educationevolving.org. You'll see the cover of *Trusting Teachers*. A click there will show you where the book is available.

Innovation-based Systemic Reform

1950s

1980s

2010s **?**

How to Get Beyond Traditional School

e e education|evolving   April 2010

Education|Evolving issued this report in 2010; its cover contrasting the dramatic change in communications with the incremental change in schooling. More than one person pointed out that the iPhone had become more than a telephone—and wondered what comparable innovation might go into the lower-right-hand corner.

A Split Screen Strategy
Creating the Capacity for Teachers to Innovate

ee education evolving

In 2012, as its thinking was clarifying about the split screen strategy, Education|Evolving produced this video of a teacher in a district near Saint Paul who individualized his third-grade classroom. It is a fascinating personal story . . . pedagogical story . . . policy story, summarized briefly in Chapter 8, page 79. To watch the video go to educationevolving.org/pai.

Creating the Capacity for Change, in 2004, saw the need for new dynamics to turn K-12 into a self-improving system. It proposed and argued for several of these: for choice, for chartering, for self-governed district schools. But 10 years ago we were only beginning to see the need to emphasize innovation in the new schools being created, chartered and district.

Copies are available from Education Week Press.

CREATING
How and Why Governors and
the CAPACITY
Legislatures Are Opening a
for CHANGE
New-Schools Sector in Public Education

TED KOLDERIE

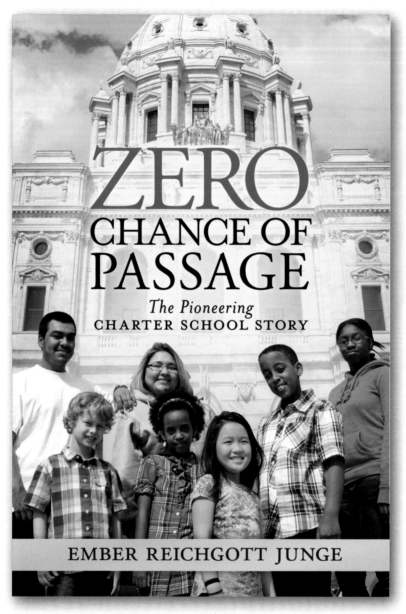

ZERO
CHANCE OF
PASSAGE
The Pioneering
CHARTER SCHOOL STORY

EMBER REICHGOTT JUNGE

Zero Chance of Passage is the definitive account of the origins of chartering; Ember Reichgott Junge's account of her involvement as a state senator in Minnesota first in inter-district open enrollment and—beginning in 1988—her effort to add a chartered sector to public education. (A professor of political science would find it an outstanding case study of legislative process and politics.) Note especially the concluding Commentary by Louise Sundin, longtime president of the Minneapolis Federation of Teachers.

Amazon sells the book. Or order on zerochanceofpassage.com

What really is 'teacher effectiveness'?

A move toward professionalism is essential because the current 'reform' effort aimed at teachers, teacher quality and teacher effectiveness is a growing concern.

There are, to be sure, problems on the 'teaching' side of public education. K-12 can hardly be called a successful system when half of those entering teaching leave within five years. It is a concern that teaching no longer draws top-level college students. New teachers themselves complain that the schools of education do not prepare them well to deal with the realities they find on the job. A sense has developed that while it is legitimate for the teacher unions to work to advance their members' interests, some of what they have won over the years is not in the student interest, and so not in the public interest, and should now be modified.

The effort to do something about teachers, teacher training and teacher accountability has been sharpened by the—now widespread—conviction that nothing matters more for student learning than having a good teacher; that students who have two or more ineffective teachers in a row are permanently disadvantaged. A belief in the importance of teacher-effectiveness has almost replaced the faith in standards as the driver of the improvement effort.

So the cry arises to find the good teachers and to weed out the 'bad'. To evaluate teachers. To get tough. To hold teachers accountable. To link compensation to student performance (defined as test scores, of course). To revise tenure and reduce union influence. These efforts now make up a significant part of contemporary 'school reform'. Not surprisingly teachers—and their unions—are pushing back. A huge conflict is developing.

It is potentially a tragedy, because the standard-enlightened notions about 'teacher quality' are seriously off-target—are probably dangerous—in several respects.

How can it not be obvious that:

» The notion of teachers being effective or ineffective, the notion of an individual teacher being good or not-good in the absolute, is too simplistic. Students differ. Some teachers are good with bright students and not with 'slow' students. Some like to work in special education; some probably are terrible there. Some are of the same race and culture as their students; some are not. On and on.[36]

» The popular notion of teacher-effectiveness ignores not only the type of students with which the teacher works but also the setting in which the teacher works. It looks only at the personal characteristics of the teacher; at his or her skill, intelligence, training, commitment. It carries no sense that a teacher's effectiveness is affected—determined, even—by the role given to the teacher; by the culture of the school or by the leadership of the school.

» The push to get 'better people for the job' fails to see the need to make teaching a better job and better career for its people. There are two efforts to raise the quality of entrants into teaching. One looks toward alternate routes to certification, works (like Teach for America) to attract top students from top colleges and universities, who have not come through the conventional teacher-preparation programs. The other looks to toughen the work in the schools preparing teachers and the requirements for admission and for certification. Neither solves the problem perceived by

---

36. When principal at Susan Lindgren Elementary in St. Louis Park MN Harry Hoff one year decided to let parents choose their child's teacher. Teachers worried that on sign-up night they would be standing at the classroom door with no one walking in. In the event, no problem: All the classrooms filled. Different students; different teachers.

the candidates: that teaching does not offer the rewards
that justify a greater investment of time and money in
additional preparation. Rewards—financial rewards—
are better in business, in medicine, in law and in other
professions. Education has no hope of equaling those
financial rewards, with three million teachers. Even if
salaries were differentiated—as in a hospital, where
only a few people are M.D.s—the additional financing
would probably go beyond what legislatures could
politically manage. The more practical solution, quite
obviously, is to upgrade the *non*-monetary rewards;
in plain words, to make teaching a better job and a
better career.

Teaching is, in truth, not a very good job and not a
very good career today. "Candidly", Arley Gunderman,
an elementary school principal in Mounds View (and
at the time a recent past-president of his national
association) told a Minnesota Business Partnership
meeting in 1984, "my job as a principal is to motivate,
as much as I can for as long as I can, people who are
in essentially dead-end jobs". If conventional reform
continues to make a career in teaching *less* attractive,
why would any reasonable person expect 'better people'
to line up in greater numbers for it?

» The 'accountability' pressure will only intensify
teacher resistance. With teachers and their unions on
the defensive politically the advocates of 'reform' are
for the moment encouraged. But teachers like most
reasonable people are unlikely to let themselves be held
accountable for decisions made by somebody else. They
will say: "If you in the central office and on the board
are going to make the decisions about how students
are to learn then *you* be accountable for student
performance". That is unlikely to succeed: Relatively

few board members or superintendents resign because students are not learning. If management says to the teachers: You are accountable for doing what I tell you to do, then teachers can exercise their option to quit.

» Turnover, already high, can get worse. Retention has always been the problem, as Richard Ingersoll of the University of Pennsylvania has shown. Twenty years ago the modal teacher in America was in his/her 15th year of work. Today, he reports, the modal teacher is in her *first* year of work.[37]

» The talk about 'better teaching' needs to ask: *"What's teaching?"*[38] No doubt there is a concept of doing better with traditional whole-class instruction; the teacher in high school at the blackboard working algebra problems, or in elementary school sitting, reading, with students grouped around. That picture expresses the conventional view of teaching. The critical question is: In the new digital environment, what *is* teaching? Is it 'better classroom management'? Or will 'better teaching' now mean knowing how to personalize, knowing how to lead project-based learning; knowing what's available online, having skills in counseling, advising and coaching?

The current proposals to link teacher compensation to student scores is contributing to the controversy about testing. Trying to bring sense to that discussion, some argue that testing in education should be what testing is in medicine: diagnostic, to give the professional an understanding of a person's condition, a

---

37. The teacher force is becoming more female, Ingersoll reports.
38. A few years ago Microsoft ran a "We See" ad pitching "software that helps kids of all ages and circumstances develop their creativity". The ad showed elementary students in a room with desks, chairs and a blackboard; showed no teacher but no computer.

sense for the treatment indicated and a measure of the progress of treatment.

But that argument struggles against the pressure for accountability; the desire of those in conventional reform to use scores as the measure of *teacher* performance. As a friend in a business organization wrote: "The only way you will get (business people) to see testing as primarily a teaching tool is to convince them that teachers aren't going to let anyone graduate who is not proficient at reading, writing and math".

Along with the effort to hold the teacher accountable goes an effort to manage teachers' work; a centralization that is tightening-down on teachers, telling them what to do and how to do it. In some districts this is 'managed instruction' in others, 'focused instruction'. One way or another it means scripting teachers' work. Good teachers dislike that; more and more do quit.

In addition to the efforts to roll back tenure there are efforts to create non-union organizations for teachers; like the Association of American Educators. Some people are predicting, perhaps hoping, that the expansion of 'digital learning' will at last undercut the teacher union control over 'supply'.[39]

For the moment the teachers and their unions are resisting; giving ground as slowly as possible. Some of their supporters seem to believe the pressure for accountability would go away if testing could be stopped. That is unlikely. The unions need a strategy.

They lack one. Resisting the pressure for accountability, criticizing 'excessive testing', appealing for more time and more training to deal with the new standards, is not a winning position. Certainly the union leadership has to be concerned that a Democratic national administration is buying the conventional reform thinking about 'teacher quality'.

All of this is dumb. We have to get out of this box.

---

39. See John Chubb and Terry Moe, *Liberating Learning: Technology, Politics, and the Future of American Education.*

This country could cut a different deal with its teachers

Start with the understanding—which should be obvious—that the behavior of teachers and unions is predictable given the incentives created for them by the arrangement in which they work.

Tradition and law blocked teachers out of decisions about curriculum and pedagogy; about learning. 'Professional issues' have been a management right. When lobbying for the Minnesota Education Association Gene Mammenga said to me: "We argue about economic issues because that's all you let us argue about". When the California Teachers Association got the Legislature to approve a bill to let teachers bargain 'professional issues' the union found a Democratic governor, Gray Davis, vetoing it; siding with the school boards.

Still, teachers were for years left pretty much alone. The basic deal this country had with its teachers was essentially: We don't-give-you professional autonomy and in return you don't-give-us accountability.

Now the new 'school reform' is changing that original deal: It proposes to hold teachers accountable for student performance *while still not giving them authority over what matters for student performance*.

It seems obvious the way out is to cut a new deal with the teachers: If you will accept responsibility for student and school success we *will* give you authority over what matters for student and school success.

1. The old deal: Teachers don't get professional authority but aren't held accountable.

2. The 'reform' deal: Teachers still don't get professional authority but *are* held accountable.

3. The 'no' deal: Teachers do get professional authority and are still not accountable.

4. The new deal: Teachers *have* professional authority and *are* accountable.

There are now schools in which teachers 'call the shots' and where they operate to a significant degree as a professional partnership. Where teachers do have real autonomy they change what the school has its students reading, seeing, hearing and doing. That comes through clearly in *Trusting Teachers with School Success*, by Kim Farris-Berg and Edward J. Dirkswager. So far the indications are that in this arrangement students learn, and that given professional authority teachers do accept accountability. There turns out to be strength in the group; importantly, more continuity than in schools using the single-leader model.

Trying, testing, collective responsibility is easier in the chartered sector where schools are more autonomous. But partnerships are appearing in the district sector as well, as in Denver's Mathematics and Science Leadership Academy—started actually by the leadership of the teachers' union. It is significant the way interest is rising in significant sectors of the teacher-union movement, both in having a larger professional role and in the partnership idea.

Professionalization was Albert Shanker's goal when he set out to unionize teaching. Eric Premack remembers that when he was a graduate student at the University of Chicago Shanker visited the school; told him he saw bargaining as a way-station on the road to professionalism.

Louise Sundin, for years on the American Federation of Teachers executive committee, took Shanker seriously. While president of the Minneapolis Federation of Teachers she tried again and again to work with the district administration to create schools in which teachers would have professional roles. Again and again she saw these schools turn back into traditional district-run schools.

In 2010 she and the current leadership of the MFT created a nonprofit that applied to become—and in 2012 was approved to be—an authorizer of new schools under Minnesota's chartering law. In testimony to the Minnesota Senate in 2011 she explained how they had been driven to the conclusion that if there are ever going to be schools that offer teachers professional roles, teachers are going to have to create them. The Minnesota Guild of Public Charter Schools is now setting out to do that; understanding, too, that as the schools become the teachers' schools there will be an associated change in the role of the union.

The partnership is more than the preferred vehicle for the professional role for teachers. It can also change learning for the students.

In the 1980s Ruth Anne Olson (whose vision this was) met with the math teachers from a big high school in the Rosemount/ Apple Valley district. The question was: Suppose you were given the resources for the math program, could select the curriculum and decide the approach to learning, were accountable for results and could keep for use in the program or as personal income what you did not need to spend. The question is not whether you'd like to do that. Just suppose that arrangement were in effect. *What would begin to happen?*

The teachers took a moment to think, then began to answer. We'd get students working individually as fast as they could go. We'd get students helping other students. We'd get parents helping as much as they could, probably at the home end. If one of us left we'd consider reallocating the duties; perhaps bring in a paraprofessional. And (this was in the 1980s, remember) we'd use whatever is available in digital electronics; computers.

What more would we be looking for? And here it is, coming from the teachers, driven by that different 'deal'. Why would we not take them up on that offer? Why would we not at least see if it would work?

Actually it is being tried, and it does work, as *Trusting Teachers* suggests. In April 2010 Carrie Bakken from Avalon School in Saint Paul and Brenda Martinez from ALBA in Milwaukee went to Washington, and in the Secretary of Education's large conference room explained to Arne Duncan and his top staff how in the partnership arrangement they make decisions, arrange the learning, manage the school and its finances and recruit, select, evaluate, compensate and when necessary terminate teachers.

So far partnerships have appeared at the whole-school level. That is the opportunity provided by chartering. But handling the whole school involves the teachers in the administration and management of the school as well as in the learning. Alternatively, teachers in a large secondary school—while continuing to be district employees—could form a partnership to handle the math department, the science department or the English department. They could then focus on learning; the principal would handle the school administration. A partnership of teachers might also organize to take responsibility for a program serving several schools across a district; Montessori, for example.

Helping the partnership idea spread

Through all its revisions Minnesota law has carried forward the provision that "The teacher shall have the general control and government of the school". Clearly that dates from the era of the one-room schoolhouse. Today, in the era of large district schools, it seems a quaint idea, obsolete and irrelevant. *But what if we now took it seriously?*

Teachers in fact appear interested and willing. In 2003 Public Agenda asked teachers "How interested would you be in working in a charter school run and managed by teachers themselves?" The question asked teachers to indicate an interest in 'charter schools' before they could reach the question of 'run and managed by teachers'. Still, 58 per cent said they would be somewhat or very interested; *two-thirds of the under-five-year teachers and half the over-20-year teachers.* Even stronger interest is visible in research done late in 2013 by Widmeyer Communications for Education|Evolving.

The partnership model needs to be further expanded, in the innovative chartered schools and hopefully in site-managed schools in the district sector.

Let's think about who does that, and how.

PART THREE

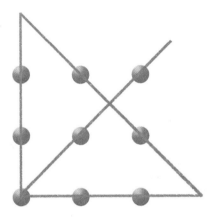

IMPLEMENTING

CHAPTER 10

Think perhaps of a 'skunk works'

The new and different approaches to learning and models of school, will come from the bottom up—as schools in both the chartered and the district sectors fight for autonomy.
It will be an unorthodox process of change. But some powerful forces will be supporting it.

It should be fairly easy to create a modest sector in K-12 in which schools and teachers can try ideas outside the traditional givens in their search for what works with individual students.

It shouldn't require major new legislation. And should be feasible politically. The split screen strategy is a moderate solution. It is hard to see who might be offended except those still trying to change everything at once, or those who want no change at all, or those insisting that their concept of the future—system and school—is the only way.

That it 'should' be easy does not of course mean it will be easy—given the notion of education policy as a search for consensus on a comprehensive transformation to be politically engineered. With mainline policy now defaulted to 'continuous improvement', the critical need will be to explain and justify the proposal to have some innovative schools operating basically as a 'skunk works'.

Successful systems offer the precedent. Business firms have set up such operations when convinced their innovators need to escape the home office with its culture of 'this is the way we've always done things'. IBM is often cited; having set up in Florida, away from the corporate headquarters, the group charged to design the personal computer.

The innovation sector can contain both charter and district

Chartering offered, and in key respects still offers, the best opportunity for the 'skunk works'. Creating autonomous schools in the district sector will be harder—but still perhaps possible.

In the chartered sector

The chartering laws leave open the questions about the kind of school to be created; about its approach to learning and about its form of organization. The opportunity there for innovation is threatened today, however, mainly by the puritans working to impose on all chartered schools their orthodoxy about learning, with its constricted definition of school design and student success.

It is fine for these people to create such schools: It is not acceptable for them, convinced of their righteousness, to block others working to create different schools. The puritans mean well, but their notion of change looks backward; focuses single-mindedly on doing traditional school better than the big urban districts. It does not look toward the new approaches to learning now possible and toward the broader kinds of achievement now needed.

So their influence is a problem. Still, assuming new schools can be shielded from their orthodoxy, the chartered sector offers major potential for innovation.

In the district sector

A 'school corporation' like a business corporation might find it helpful to have an R&D sector. Creating even a few schools different from its 'regular schools', able to test new approaches, would create useful dynamics within the organization.

Business firms other than IBM have used this model as the route into a different future. A conspicuous case was Dayton-Hudson Corporation, which did this by setting up its discount operation in a different corporation managed by different executives at a different location.[40] Discounting was in effect competing with the corporation's department stores. But, as Douglas Dayton explained: "When we sat as the board of the parent company, we could hardly complain."

Might a district do the same? In most states chartering offers districts this opportunity. And some districts *have* tried to use chartering this way. In some states the decentralization statutes provide an alternate path. Minnesota law provides for 'site-based' and more recently for 'self-governed' schools. Boston—Massachusetts' chartering law not being available to districts—created its own 'Pilot Schools'.

Who's for Innovation?

Within the district sector several parties might find an interest in innovation.

Boards of education

In Colorado in 1993 the state school boards association opposed the chartering legislation—which did pass. Later that year its executive, Randy Quinn, suggested to his members that

---

40. In his Harvard Business Review article early in 2000, "Meeting the Challenge of Disruptive Change", Clayton Christensen noted that out of the hundreds of full-line department store companies only one made the transition successfully into discounting. This was Dayton-Hudson; today, Target Corporation.

for school boards chartering could be "a blessing in disguise"; a way to respond to differences of opinion within the district by "establishing schools of different types".[41]

In Mounds View, a district north of Saint Paul, the area learning center (ALC)—an alternative school—applied in 1992 for charter status. Privately the district's attorney saw this as a solution: The ALC had been pressing to be different, to serve its 'different' students. That made sense, but the central office worried that "If we let you do it the high school will want to do it, too". Move the ALC to charter status, he said, where it could make its own decisions to do-different, and the board would not be setting the precedent.

Teachers seeking professional status

About 2000 a van carrying teachers from Milwaukee visited New Country School, a chartered secondary school at Henderson, Minnesota using a project-based approach to learning and operating as a workers' cooperative. The Milwaukee teachers liked the school; liked especially the idea of it being the teachers' school.

Cris Parr was at the time a 17-year veteran of the Milwaukee schools and the union representative in most where she taught. Wanting to create a school like that in Milwaukee, she went to her father. John Parr had for years headed the AFSCME local in Milwaukee, in which capacity he had bargained for the clericals in the district. The superintendent, Bill Andrekopoulos, was supportive. So Cris Parr was able to create the I.D.E.A.L. school, a K-8 elementary.

Wisconsin's original chartering law is a kind of site-management law, the school remaining legally an "instrumentality of the district" and the teachers remaining employees of the district. In time Cris created two other schools, and with her father's help

---

41. I asked Quinn how and when this came to him. "I began to see it during the legislative debate", he said.

other teachers created eight or nine more. The schools negotiated memoranda of understanding with the district and the union that delegated significant authority to the school; particularly the right to evaluate their own people and flexibility in the use of time; day, week and year.

In other cities, too, teachers are moving to start schools or to take control of schools. In 2012 Education|Evolving selected about a dozen such schools; looked to see what happens, what changes, when teachers 'call the shots. This is the research that produced *Trusting Teachers.*

Progressive superintendents

Good superintendents feel coerced by the pressure for 'sameness'.[42] They know students differ; know the needs for learning differ. They accept the need to try things. If they could proceed one school at a time they might be able to make significant change.

Some of this is visible now in Minnesota. Lisa Snyder, superintendent in Lakeville, has let teachers open the K-3 Impact Academy as a school basically operated by the teachers. When support for a chartered school was not forthcoming in Staples-Motley, Superintendent Mark Schmitz opened Connections Academy as a district school. Mark Bezik in Elk River will open a similar school in September 2014.

Unions, seeing the need for professional status for their members

There are things union locals can do within the district structure to help members interested in larger professional roles. Success will not require action by all or even a majority of the teachers: If a few start more will follow. What's important is to get started.

---

42. Listen to Tom Nelson talking about the internal pressures for uniformity, in http://www.educationevolving.org/pai.

Albert Shanker encouraged AFT locals to put proposals into the bargaining process.[43] Louise Sundin, then heading the Minneapolis Federation of Teachers, began pushing against the disinclination of the board to bargain on policy questions. More recently in Saint Paul Mary Cathryn Ricker has been doing the same in her role as president of the AFT local there. Early in 2014 she bargained into the new contract with the Saint Paul board an agreement about class size, traditionally considered a policy matter for management, and a provision allowing an individual school to initiate 'micro-bargaining' with the district for what they now call a 'redesign' of the school.

The potential alliance for personalizing learning

STUDENT	TEACHERS
"My skills, my aptitudes My interests"	"We know our students as individuals"
PERSONALIZE INDIVIDUALIZE CUSTOMIZE	
"Our capability, our potential"	"My child!"
DIGITAL SOFTWARE	PARENTS

This irritates boards of education, which insist that 'policy' and 'professional issues' are a management right. But "a bargain-

43. See his address in April 1985 at the AFT meeting in Niagara Falls; "The Making of a Profession".

able issue is whatever one party insists on making a bargainable issue", Sam Romer used to advise when labor reporter for the Minneapolis Tribune. What if teachers *make* professionalization and policy-change a bargainable issue?

The whole process would be greatly eased and speeded were some honest broker to get union and management leadership together on the 'new deal' for teachers discussed in Chapter 9: to give teachers the authority over what matters for student and school success, in return for which teachers accept responsibility for student and school success.[44]

'Coming full circle'

Teachers can move into the chartered sector as individuals to work in new schools—or to start new schools. Teachers—even union leadership—can organize authorizing bodies to create new schools. This is what the leadership of the Minneapolis Federation did in creating the Guild in 2012. This decision to go into chartering is what Louise Sundin called "coming full circle" in the commentary she wrote for *Zero Chance of Passage*, Ember Reichgott Junge's account of the origins of chartering.

TURN, the Teacher Union Reform Network, has been thinking and talking about this idea now for six or more years. When it met in Minneapolis in October 2012 the group—elected presidents and staff from locals in both the AFT and NEA—brought in teachers ('advisers') from a partnership school. The AFT innovation fund has financed the start-up of the Guild in Minnesota. On the NEA side John Wright and Bill Raabe are assigned to this idea.

---

44. See page 92.

Here're a few of the opportunities for teachers to push to expand their role. Some, perhaps most, are present in some form in most states.

Look for the statutes that provide for school-based decision-making or for site-governed schools.

Look for the opportunities in their state's chartered sector. Hopefully there are multiple authorizers; at least one of these soliciting or welcoming proposals for schools that aim to get outside the traditional givens.

Look at the so-called innovation statutes present in some states. These might require the school to get permission for specific changes. But it's worth seeing what's possible. If nothing else, simply applying—and publicizing the application—will be useful.

Here and there a school, or even a single teacher, might take the initiative to do-different—on the theory that it's better to ask forgiveness than permission. Chapter 8 told about the teacher in the district near Saint Paul who acted on his own to personalize his third-grade classroom. The conversion was not expensive: Many charities could, if asked, provide the $6,000 required.

Beyond this, look for ways to create more opportunities for innovation. Get into the policy discussion, at all levels—as the new organization that calls itself Educators 4 Excellence says it proposes to do.

Powerful drivers will encourage innovation

Because people will think first of the obstacles to innovation, it is important to underscore the important factors and important actors likely to support it.

Certain underlying forces will have a substantial effect.

» **The general 'unbundling' of services**—Across many if not most fields the old standardized model of service has been breaking down. More and more choices are now being offered. Think how diverse the state's program of public education has become: district schools, inter-district enrollment, chartered schools, some state-run specialized schools, 'alternative' schools, online learning.

» **The appeal of personalization**—The spread of the digital electronics and the new social media make clear that learning can be adapted to the needs and interests of the individual student: See Chapter 8. Some research now also says that maximizing achievement requires starting with the attainment-level of the individual student: See Jack Frymier's comments in Chapter 5. This will call for innovation both in pedagogy and in assessment. 'Adaptive' assessment is now appearing; software that gives the test-taker progressively harder questions if she is answering most questions correctly, and easier questions if she is answering most questions incorrectly . . . until it finds the top of the student's attainment level in both cases.

» **The effort to make teaching 'a better job for its people'**—Chapter 9 talked about the challenge of attracting top candidates into teaching when its monetary rewards are insufficient to persuade top candidates to choose teaching over other fields. It looked to making teaching a rewarding job and career by enlarging teachers' professional role. Trusting teachers with school and student success will open opportunities for them to innovate; to try new approaches to learning; to change the technology of learning.[45]

» **The push to centralize and standardize might fall of its own weight**—The sense seems to be growing that conventional education policy has not made adequate progress. Though intense efforts are now being made to save it, the plan to introduce the Common Core standards and assessments is encountering serious resistance from those who argue that what's tested will inevitably become what's taught. There is a continuing desire out there for diverse approaches.

» **Finally, perhaps, simple common sense**—Over and over this book has suggested the standard theology of education policy falls short in many ways. This might come increasingly to be recognized. Hopefully, too, those pushing improvement-within-the-givens will take to heart the caution about the way that one-bet strategy puts the nation at risk.

Some powerful actors are likely to be working for innovation.

» **Teacher and teacher unions, local and national.** These can lead in creating the innovation sector. Schools and teachers are the actors marginalized by the prevailing theory of action that looks to policy and to 'leadership' with its presumed ability to change K-12 'comprehensively'. An active effort by teachers

---

45. The popular media have been reporting on 'crowdsourcing', online marketplaces in which teachers sell their curriculum ideas, their lesson plans, to teachers nationwide. One, TeachersPayTeachers, was started in 2006 by a former New York middle-school teacher. See Andy Rotherham's column in *Time* September 20, 2012.

and unions to win professional status . . . to get the authority to control what matters for student and school success . . . could almost by itself secure the establishment of the Innovation sector on the split screen. Such teacher initiative would represent a kind of rebellion. *But that is the way paradigms change . . . discontented professionals offering new perspectives; challenging 'the way we've always done things'.*

» **The software industry.** Innovation should create significant new markets for digital software. It might be a challenge to interest some firms in marketing to individual schools, let alone to individual teachers. But in this large and complex industry there will likely be some vendors interested in moving to this opportunity.

» **The media, spreading information about new models.** 'The new' always interests the media. With its short time-horizon journalism has a hard time keeping in perspective the slow and uneven progress of innovation. It tends to move quickly from "Gee-Whiz" to "Gosh-Awful"; from stories about great intentions to stories about disappointing results. Worse, it has bought in to the simplistic notion of student performance as scores-on-tests.[46] Fundamentally, though, the media is in the 'news' business, and happily we are now seeing more coverage of innovations—perhaps because of the disappointment with conventional strategy. Can you imagine the reporters covering the auto industry, for example, writing just about improvements in conventional cars and paying no attention to hybrid or electric vehicles?

---

46. For a time some education reporters were assigned to an 'accountability' beat; covering test scores.

» Researchers. They have tended not to be interested in single cases of new-and-different, preferring to generalize about 'what works'. That focus on replication is appropriate for the improvement side of the split screen. But it will be important to have some research attentive to the single cases of new-and-different; perhaps following up on what journalism brings to its attention. The split screen strategy, the effort to get education to change the way successful systems change, depends on information about innovative models reaching others potentially interested.

» Students and parents. It is good to remember that the chartering laws created no schools; simply enabled their creation. The schools were created by the unexpected outpouring of effort by ordinary people: parents, community groups and teachers. Who can say whether the range of schools created so far in the chartered sector has yet fully satisfied that latent desire for different and better learning opportunities for America's children? Parents who understand the differences among their children will want appropriately different kinds of learning. Students themselves want to be successful and not to be bored.

What are the specific 'action steps'?

There is no one action that will open the innovation side of the split screen. It will appear as teachers and schools try things. In truth, the innovation sector might already be appearing, as more and more individual schools begin to test new approaches to learning and new forms of organization, breaking with one or more of the givens of conventional school.

The challenge is to get more schools innovating—and to make sure that is not suppressed by the pressures to draw all schools back into the traditional form.

The change will be slow; two steps forward; a step back: That is the way innovation proceeds. In Colorado not many district boards took up Randy Quinn's suggestion that chartering could help them diversify their offerings. In Mounds View the board and superintendent turned down the application from the ALC. And as Richard Kahlenberg concedes in his biography, most of the AFT locals did not respond to Albert Shanker's push for professionalism; did not at the time show significant interest in moving beyond traditional bargaining.

Those were the initial efforts, though; in the 1980s and '90s. People keep trying; keep pushing. And gradually their initiatives begin to succeed. The question is how these can be expanded.

A first obvious step is for those who practice and who support innovation to meet and talk about the idea of the split screen strategy; to find and agree on ways to advance it; to organize toward this objective.

This much seems clear:

» Innovation will come in significant part as schools and teachers practice insubordination; as they break with the traditional givens and introduce new ways of doing things without first asking permission.

» The innovations will come at small scale, in individual schools broadly dispersed across the sectors and around the country.

» It will be easier in the chartered sector, but that effort should be made in the district sector as well.

» Real innovation will require real autonomy, a meaningful delegation to schools and teachers of the authority to break with the conventional givens and to adapt learning to the needs and to the situation of the students they know.

» As always, most change will come from the challenge of discontented professionals rather than from those inside established organizations.

Let's consider next what this implies for state and national policymakers. Their role will be critical. But it will be different from what is currently conceived.

CHAPTER 11

What role for state and national policy?

Begin with the understanding that the states do not run the schools and that Washington cannot structure the K-12 system in the states. For state and national policymakers the key to change will be leadership and persuasion.

The state—the governor as chief executive for the education enterprise and the legislature as its board of directors—should move to the split screen strategy for change. The challenge for the state will be to find a way to get the autonomy needed for innovation into a significant number of schools and to their teachers.

The state makes the system. Almost everywhere in this country education is a state responsibility. State constitutions charge the legislature to create a 'general and uniform' or 'thorough and efficient' system of public schools. The state arranges the financing. And the state reserves to itself the power to change the system: Education lacks the concept of 'home rule' that exists for municipalities (and more recently, in some states, for counties).

But the state does not create or run the schools. Its law provides for citizens, local voters, to create districts that will set up and run the schools. Nor does the state appoint the officials who run the district schools: Local voters elect boards of education that appoint the superintendents and select the principals who run the schools. In most of America these are independent special districts that stand outside general local government. In the states K-12 is organized legally and operates politically on the principle of 'local control'.

Beginning in 1991 states added a charter sector to the system. But in this new sector as well, the state does not run the schools or appoint the officials who do.

So, as the sense develops that the institution needs to do better, and to be more innovative, the question for state policy leadership is: How do we get change and improvement in a system we do not own and do not directly control?

The impulse is to mandate change and improvement; some 'best way'. There is much brave talk about holding districts accountable. But the truth is that none of the state efforts has been notably effective: not exhortation, not technical support and not 'more money'—popular though that always is. Mandates are resisted, sometimes fiercely, and are used anyway more for conformity than for change: Certainly it is difficult to mandate innovation.

As the effort to 'make 'em improve' continues to disappoint, the states continue to search for an alternative strategy.

California is now an important state to watch. Its state education code has grown to about 5,600 pages; the state telling districts what to do and how to do it and even selecting textbooks. Now Governor Jerry Brown and the Legislature have decided that 40 years of strong central control has not been effective. They mean now to back away; mean to delegate greater flexibility and authority to the state's roughly 1,000 districts.

But for them, too, the question is how to ensure the districts use the new authority and financial flexibility in the interest of the students; in improving learning—without the state again resorting to mandates. How will they do that?

The split screen strategy is arguably the answer

A state cannot enact decentralization: It is up to the districts to move authority into the schools. But states can pass legislation enabling districts to give their schools real authority to change and to innovate. And the states can urge districts to use that enabling legislation.

Again, at this level, the question is: How?

Probably the answer is for state superintendents and commissioners to recognize the influence they can exert without the power to command. They can emphasize the need for school and teacher autonomy and can point to what has been done elsewhere. They can emphasize and publicize the need to personalize learning. They can do research, keep records and document success and failure. They can speak directly to teachers, urging them to ask their districts for that meaningful delegation of real authority.[47]

Let's look at four possible state actions.

1. **Reaffirm the idea of chartering as the principal innovation sector of the split screen strategy. Perhaps enact a 'Chartering 2.0' that contains even broader opportunities for change.**

Over the 15 or more years these laws have been in effect most have accumulated barnacles. The original idea was for these schools to be accountable for results rather than for process. But regulations enacted for the district sector came to be applied to the chartered schools as well—contrary to the original intent.

Legislatures might now scrape off these barnacles, removing regulations and returning to the original concept of chartering as innovation. They might charge some authorizers explicitly to

---

47. In Minnesota in 1987 Governor Rudy Perpich wrote the district superintendents, urging them to open to non-residents under the state's new program of inter-district choice.

solicit innovative proposals, as does Innovative Quality Schools, a single-purpose authorizer in Minnesota.

Perhaps a two-part chartered sector would be appropriate: one for the kind of 'high-performing', high-scoring schools pushed by the CMOs and another specifically for schools that emphasize innovation. The latter might be given longer terms. (In his initial thinking about 'charter schools' Albert Shanker talked about giving the teachers five or 10 years to show what they could do.)

> **2. In the district sector push the school-based decision-making laws so they will operate successfully. Or go to 'divestiture'.**

Minnesota in recent years has been 'encouraging' districts to make a real delegation of meaningful authority to schools that request it. Districts, however, remain reluctant to grant this autonomy. Their impulse toward uniformity, toward sameness, is strong. Sensing this, schools are reluctant to seek autonomy.

Financial incentives come to mind. But these are overrated. In 1973 Joe Graba, then a state representative in Minnesota, helped create the Council on Quality Education, essentially a state foundation financing innovation. Ten years later, as deputy commissioner, he helped shut it down. There were good ideas. But what was financed did not last and did not spread.

Perhaps—at least in large districts—a better answer is to do the divestiture proposed in Chapter 3. Moving certain districts from the bureau model to the contract model will not by itself get authority into the school. But it can at least create the conditions essential for that delegation of autonomy.

This concept of 'creating the conditions for change' should be the heart of the state's strategy. John Goodlad put it perfectly in *Educational Renewal* in 1994. When people see something working, Goodlad wrote, the impulse is to say, "Bottle it!" That is, to take the new (whatever) and show it to, sell it to, other schools and districts. 'Bottle it!' is the replication we so commonly see.

Wrong, Goodlad said: Rather, *identify the conditions responsible for producing the good new idea and replicate those conditions* in other schools. The 'conditions' have mainly to do with enabling schools to control what matters for learning and, in the school, leaving good teachers alone to do what they know how to do.[48]

Alternatively, a state might reasonably consider an 'opt-out' program. This would make it possible for an existing school to leave its district if it wished and to join a small 'sub-system' of schools contracted directly to the state. That would create some significant incentives; would tell a district that saying 'no' to a school asking to go self-governed would not terminate the school's interest or its ability to become autonomous.

Creating a small sector contracted directly to the state would also activate an important issue about how the state oversees innovation.

3. Move the 'innovation' sector away from the state agency.

Over the years the state education agency has become increasingly regulatory. In any bureaucracy the tradition is to preserve the existing state of affairs; in a state education agency that means ensuring that schools do not depart from the rules. This is fatal for real innovation. A governor and legislature wanting to develop an effective R&D sector for their public education will have to come to grips with this problem.

Conceivably the answer might be a kind of 'bundling board' dividing the agency internally—below the level of the commissioner (or state superintendent)—into a regulatory side and an innovation side. But it asks a lot of the chief state school officer

---

48. Goodlad warned early about the dangers of the accountability model. System reform sounds attractive, he wrote in Chapter 7, page 204ff, but quickly turns into "target-directed, linear approaches that traditional rationality dictates . . . is transformed into a tightening-up of the ends/means connections among outcomes, a curriculum to deliver these, and tests to measure them." Prophetic.

to run two different operations in the same organizational structure.

So it might be safer, more effective, to create a separate entity. Then the state would be—in Clayton Christensen's terms—"running two different *enterprises* at the same time". A governor probably could by executive order put the innovation— or opt-out—program into some incubator somewhere in state government, possibly in the executive office itself. (Note that in some states governors have had a 'secretary of education' who was not the chief state school officer.)

4. Try running full financing to the student.

A core idea of public education is to provide—to make available and to pay for—a quality education for the student. Over the years, as choice has spread, the states have let public financing follow the student to more and more different kinds of schools: to the schools of a nearby district . . . to a college or university under a post-secondary option . . . to a chartered school . . . generally, to entities operating on the essential principles of public education.

With the appearance now of learning programs available over the Internet, there comes a question whether to extend the definition of 'the school' further. 'School' might no longer be a place at all; might be the student working at any location. Students, gathered together 'virtually' by a teacher or group of teachers, might 'go to school' online.

Virtual schools could operate outside the framework of public regulation; could be truly innovative. These would not have to ask permission-in-advance for what they propose to do. They and their students would have to achieve the outcomes they said they would achieve. They would be accountable for those results and for using public funds honestly; would have to demonstrate they had in fact been innovative and would be subject to revocation should they fail on either dimension. The state could prohibit a religious affiliation. It could require a report on student learning at, say, the 10-year point. As a way to maximize innovative approaches to learning the idea is worth thinking about.

National policy should support the state effort at innovation

Basically this enabling strategy for the state should be the strategy also for the national government. Washington should adopt the split screen strategy, support innovation and create 'conditions' that induce the states to move to the split screen idea themselves.

Just as the states do not run the schools the national government does not write education law. So the same question arises for Washington that arises for policy leadership at the state capitol: How do we get change and improvement in a system we do not own or control?

The same impulse to control, to mandate improvement, is present in the national discussion.

By 2000, just before 9/11 changed national priorities, the polls were showing 'education' to be the public's number-one concern. Because elected officials want to be seen responding to what concerns the public, a problem identified everywhere in the country became 'a national problem'—with the inference that 'a national problem' required action by the national government.

In Congressional politics the measure of commitment had long been the level of financing. Because Democrats would always trump what Republicans were willing to spend, education came to be seen as 'a Democratic issue'. But in the 2000 campaign, in a brilliant political stroke, Republicans used 'accountability' to trump money, capturing the education issue. Late in 2001 the Congress then enacted President Bush's campaign slogan about 'leaving no child behind'.

"National policy comes of age" Christopher Cross subtitled his book, *Political Education*, two years later. In its introduction Richard Riley, secretary of education 1993-2001, and Ted Sanders, president at the time of the Education Commission of the States, wrote: "Clearly education is today a national issue. The genie can never be put back in the bottle".

This reflects the tendency to think of the schools being "America's schools". It is as if this country indeed had a national education system.

I went with the American delegation to Finland in August 2012. At the end of a briefing there about PISA I commented to the presenter they had not shown a ranking for 'Europe's schools'. She said what clearly she felt should have been obvious: 'Europe' does not have schools. In the same sense, I said, 'America' does not have schools.

It is a common problem in inter-national comparisons to fail to see that in areas of domestic policy like education the counterpart of the European state is the American state. A level comparison would relate Finland to Minnesota; state to state; 'America' to 'Europe'. Washington is Brussels.[49]

One afternoon recently, seeing this confusion appear in discussion about the PISA rankings, I emailed a mild complaint to Andreas Schleicher, who runs the Program for International Student Assessment for OECD in Paris. I made my argument for state-to-state comparisons. A half-hour later he wrote back: "I thoroughly agree"—and went on to say that some American states had bought into PISA's 2012 survey. He said he is happy there will now be a more detailed picture of how well the schools *in* America are doing. And the PISA results that appeared in Fall 2013 did begin to show state-to-state comparisons—on which some American states show well.

The sense of a national system, as it develops, leads those in our national government to begin to feel responsible for the problems of the schools. And, feeling responsible, they believe they

49. Even more peculiar is to compare 'America' to what are essentially not nations at all, but urban regions: Hong Kong, Shanghai.

must do something. Yet whether the national government should act directly to fix those problems is not so clear. Better, perhaps, first to consider two things that ought to be obvious:

» Though appearing everywhere in the nation, problems in domestic systems that exist in state law are not national problems in the sense that foreign relations, national defense and monetary policy are national problems.

In areas of domestic policy that exist in state law the national government's approach, going back many years, has been to assert 'national policy' by offering money to the states with regulations attached. The theory is that the states and localities will never reject the money so will accept any regulations tied to it.

Clearly this has worked; states usually do accept the regulations. Whether the regulations prove effective in producing the effect intended is another question.

Consider 'urban policy'. In the 1960s in metropolitan areas across America the old urban core was deteriorating while new development was 'sprawling' outward at the suburban fringe. Governance was, the planners liked to say, "fragmented". Nobody was in charge of the region as a whole, balancing core and fringe. Quickly this was termed 'a national problem'. And quickly it was assumed this required action by the national government—even though most all the elements of the problem were under state jurisdiction: the laws covering land-use and zoning; the housing and building codes; the organization and financing of local government; the property-tax system; the organization of parks, streets and transit and of sewerage and water supply.

By 1966 Washington had shaped a theory of action. At its core was the idea of attaching regulations and requirements to the flow of federal aid for housing and urban renewal, for roads, transit, sewer and water systems, for parks and open space and municipal planning. As a condition of receiving federal aid every metropolitan area would be required to have a regional council.

This council would make a regional plan. All applications from local units of government for federal aid would be reviewed by the regional council for conformity to the regional plan. From this process, we were assured, orderly urban development would proceed.

It did not. Political pressure from the mayors and from county government ensured the regional councils would be composed of sitting officials of the cities and counties: The councils would be councils *of governments*; COGs, as they came to be called. No way were these local officials going to let an application for a development project in their jurisdiction be vetoed by a council trying to implement some regional plan. So the COGs became what David Walker of the Advisory Commission on Intergovernmental Relations called "paper mills"; commonly finding all applications consistent with the regional plan or never approving a plan with which a local application could not be found consistent. In 1981 the new national administration that came into office took the whole structure down.[50]

The same situation prevails with education. Education exists in state law. Local units of government run the schools. National lawmaking cannot change the structure of K-12 education or directly change what goes on in the schools. Congress is not the nation's board of education. The secretary of education is not the nation's school superintendent.

So quite possibly the current effort at 'national education policy' could meet the same fate as that effort at 'national urban policy', with people producing prescriptions that say 'must' and regulations that say 'must not' until the effort collapses of its

---

50. Washington had a hard time thinking clearly about 'the urban problem', about 'cities'. Soon after taking office as the first secretary of Housing and Urban Development (HUD) Robert Weaver, appearing at the National Press Club, was asked: "Sometimes when you talk about 'the city' you seem to mean the central municipality; sometimes you seem to be referring to the metropolitan area." Weaver scratched his head and said, "I guess we are kind of confused about that." Today HUD handles a variety of housing programs. Washington no longer tries to have a 'national urban policy'.

own weight. In 2013 the Senate committee handling education produced a bill 1,000 pages long.

> » **The logical strategy is to work through the power of state lawmaking.**

To point out the limitations of national policy in education is not to minimize the national interest in improving education or to deny the usefulness of a national role or to assert the principle of 'states' rights'. It is to emphasize the reality that Washington cannot 'fix the schools'. *Its role is to develop a strategy to activate the states to create conditions that will cause the districts and the chartering organizations to create schools that work well.*

This does *not* mean requiring the states to put into statute the regulations and rules Washington is now attaching to its grants-in-aid. Rather, it should be an effort to stimulate *creative* lawmaking; lawmaking that will get K-12 to change the way successful systems change, turning K-12 into a self-improving system.

National policy should defer to states the decisions on the way to set up and structure the new innovative sector—as the Clinton administration and the Congress in 1994, when setting up the new national program of assistance for chartering, deferred to states the decisions about who could run a school and who could authorize a school. The operating principle should be: incentives from the top down; implementation from the bottom up.

The president should speak to the states

A new dimension of presidential leadership could help enormously in leveraging the states into this new effort to redesign public education. The 'bully pulpit' role—one important model of presidential leadership—can be a critical element of the national government's strategy.

All through his time in office President Clinton gave remarkable support to the effort to introduce chartering into state law. In this he was implementing the centrist political strategy—a combination of public-school choice and chartering, in-between conventional improvement and vouchers—that Will Marshall at the Democratic Leadership Council had shaped in 1992 when working up the policy book for the incoming administration.[51]

But beyond speeches and statements a president could act directly to activate the process of state lawmaking.

Nothing in the Constitution limits a president to putting proposals only before the Congress; *nothing prevents a president from laying policy proposals before the legislatures of the states.* A president could go to an individual state legislature . . . or to any number of them . . . and to the Education Commission of the States, and to the Council of State Governments and to the National Conference of State Legislatures and to the National Governors Association and perhaps also to the Council of Chief State School Officers.

Why would a president concerned about so important a problem as public education not want to be laying proposals before the legislative bodies that have the superior capacity to act effectively to change that system?

---

51. See *Mandate for Change*. Also, Ember Reichgott Junge's account in Chapter 30 of *Zero Chance of Passage*.

CHAPTER 12

It is time to be practical

*The time has come to remember the importance of changing
what is not a winning game*

Trying endlessly to push change into an inert system makes no
basic sense. A concept of education policy built on this theory of
action does not work; is not practical.

Nor does the effort to transform the system radically through
political action succeed. It, too, is not practical. A political
majority for radical change is almost a contradiction in terms.

The strategy of 'continuous improvement' is described as
'systemic'—aiming to push at least incremental change into all
schools, gradually but 'at scale'. Still, that has not been notably
successful either. The effect—as the public sets the limited,
incremental change against its sense that learning must improve
dramatically—has been to increase discontent with the policymakers and with the schools.

Some of the changes introduced even by 'continuous improvement', as it takes the existing arrangements in K-12 as given,
ask responses from districts and schools that do not fit with the
incentives that exist in those arrangements and with the culture
created by those arrangements.[52]

---

52. Lewis Perelman offered that objection to the idea of putting computers in
    conventional classrooms. "Like putting afterburners on horses", he said. "They
    are not compatible technologies."

This of course puts back in perspective the basic question about strategy. *If K-12 is an inert system shouldn't the strategy be to find what can turn it into a self-improving system and do that?* Find what will give the schools, district and chartered, incentives to be continually searching for quality improvements and financial efficiencies; on their own initiative, in their own interest and from their own resources.

Chartering was introduced about 20 years ago in an effort to attack that systemic problem; to introduce incentives into a district system that—as Albert Shanker put it at the Itasca Seminar—could "take its customers for granted". Withdrawing the districts' exclusive was a key part of this strategy for change.

But the new-schools strategy works only if it produces innovation. A real element of innovation needs to be added to the strategy now . . . while conventional improvement continues in the mainline system.

The country, and any given state, will then be testing two different strategies at the same time. This is basic common sense. The split screen strategy is the practical approach to change.

Personalization is the place to start

The idea is to find the key that will open the door; to find "the one thing that leads on to everything else"—or, as Murnane and Levy wrote, "the initiative that creates the most pressure for other constructive changes".[53]

That "one thing that leads on to everything else" is to personalize learning. Personalization draws in the digital electronics, creating a new technology that changes both students' and teachers' roles. In so doing it increases motivation. Better motivation means better achievement. It will improve achievement. A teacher of the year in Minnesota liked to say, "Only individualized learning can leave no child behind".

---

53. *Teaching the New Basic Skills*, Richard J. Murnane and Frank Levy; page 224, citing Albert Hirschman.

What, then, is critical for personalization to appear? It is to create the conditions that let teachers adapt to the attainment-levels, aptitudes and interests of the individual student.

How, then, to do that? Offer teachers a professional role that has them working collegially in partnerships, internalizing the issues about 'effectiveness' and 'accountability' issues within their professional group. Try that innovation. Let the model spread if and as it succeeds. Let it evolve.

The split-screen is a better strategy than one that has policy-makers and managers trying to drive change into all schools at once. K-12 is a conservative institution; it will resist. The pressure for sameness remains strong. "Deviance is a struggle", Goodlad wrote in *A Place Called School* in 1985. The incentives are for everyone to standardize.

This conservatism about 'real school' is why even with the split screen the effort must be to introduce innovation at small scale; to let it grow gradually and voluntarily. Go on doing continuous improvement in existing schools; just *add to that a serious effort to stimulate innovation in autonomous schools in which teachers are trusted to adapt to the students they know.*

This process of trying things, letting new methods spread, is—again—the way successful systems change. This strategy can in time turn K-12 into a self-improving system.

Innovation could easily bypass school

In the education policy discussion, and among educators, there is some tendency to think that learning occurs only in school, and—along with this—to think that if school does not change then the new-and-different will not happen.

Nothing could be further from the truth. *If school does not open to innovation the new and non-traditional models will sweep around it.* Families that can afford the cost of learning privately can and will go outside conventional school, now that digital electronics make it possible to learn elsewhere, any time.

Harvard's Richard Elmore identifies this potential when he says, "Learning outside school is exploding; learning inside school is imploding". Or says, "This is the best time in history to be a learner—unless you happen to be in school".[54]

Only three things are needed for this bypass:

1. Ways for people to learn.

2. Someone to assess and validate what is learned.

3. A willingness to accept those validations on the part of whatever organization or institution the student wishes to enter next.

All three are appearing; all can easily develop further.

Nothing about that bypass would respect the equity principles of public education. But that would not stop its happening. Those who see themselves working to preserve 'the system'— traditional school—need to understand the dilemma they face, between 'the ethics of responsibility' and 'the ethics of ultimate ends'. Believing they are acting to stop what they oppose they risk bringing it about.

Can 'policy' lead? Or are the teachers the leaders?

It would be a major breakthrough were someone in a position of leadership—state or national, public or private—to say what is obvious; that it is time for that new deal with teachers: real authority over what matters for student and school success in return for real accountability for student and school success.

---

54. Quoted in Jal Mehta, *The Futures of School Reform*.

» Perhaps a political person aspiring to be governor, or president, will see the opportunity here.

» Union leadership might propose that authority-for-accountability deal.

» So might the Secretary of Education—perhaps in an address to one of the major education associations, to the NEA or AFT annual conventions, for example, or to the Education Commission of the States.

Just suggesting, explaining and legitimizing, the split screen idea could have a powerful effect on what policymakers do.

Failing that, the innovation side of the split screen will have to develop as teachers push for professional autonomy—in their classrooms, in their departments; in their schools; in their learning programs; insisting on adapting to their students' individual interests, aptitudes and levels of attainment as the best way to improve achievement.

It will be important for the groups now so focused on better education to support the teachers in this: the foundations, the civic organizations, the specifically 'school reform' groups, the media. Hopefully the industry designing and producing digital software will also be interested and helpful.

None of this sounds like what we normally think of as 'education policymaking': change conceived at the top, written into law, implemented 'system-wide'.

Yet all around us in recent years we have seen major social change proceeding in precisely this way: people deciding they want to do differently and 'leadership', the formal institutions, adjusting, adapting, following.

'This is not a drill'

Improving, broadening and deepening the skills of the American public—of the whole public, not only of those currently enrolled in school—is now a national imperative. We *have* to do this; *have* to succeed at this.

Increasingly economists and policy analysts point with concern to the rate at which digital electronics are disrupting businesses and industries; moving jobs and destroying jobs. The firms affected are not just the old-line businesses. The Economist recently noted that a firm making GPS devices for your car—which had disrupted the industry of conventional map-making—was then itself destroyed as cellphones added apps for GPS.

None of this is new: New machines and new methods have always destroyed jobs. New jobs, new kinds of work, have then appeared. At one time half the workers in America were farmers. Today perhaps 3 per cent farm. The others went into new kinds of work. To make this transition people had to develop new skills.

Today as the disruption moves faster the educational transformation must move faster. Our current system for educating and training people is not up to that challenge. And our current theory about how to change education is not up to that challenge. *Struggling to develop a consensus for political action, trying to make a plan for an essentially un-knowable future, we paralyze ourselves.*

We have got to break with the old givens about school and with the old process of changing school. The only practical strategy is to do as successful systems do: to open to new and radically different ways of doing—to new forms, processes and approaches—and to let those models and practices spread as rapidly as people accept them.

It is the strategy of *innovation-based* systemic reform. It is the 'split screen' idea.

ACKNOWLEDGEMENTS—
AND A PERSONAL REQUEST

Over the past 30 years I've sent memos to people I know and like and respect in the world of education policy—trying out ideas often outside the mainstream of the current discussion. I got back remarkable responses; not always positive but always thoughtful. I think of this book as another of those memos offering ideas and hopefully insights; obviously extended but still an argument, not a book of research or scholarship. I hope readers will approach it and accept it as such.

Its thinking carries on from what I wrote in 2004 in *Creating the Capacity for Change*. Looking back at that earlier book I note I began then by saying "The current theory of action contains a critical flaw". So there is continuity in the thinking.

It is customary in acknowledgements to relieve one's colleagues of responsibility for what appears. I am tempted not to do that. I have depended heavily on the experience, wisdom and judgments of my colleagues in Education|Evolving and of friends with whom I have discussed these ideas. They have taught me what I know about this field. More important: I like to think they would want to be associated even with a strategy that departs as dramatically as does this one from conventional policy thinking.

I hope those in the mainline policy discussion will take its central idea seriously. The 'split screen' approach to system change, and the proposal to make central the schools' and teachers' authority in learning, do challenge the traditional givens. Still, I hope some, at least, of those in important positions in the K-12 system will say: Yes; this is necessary; it is time.

I hope, too, that those with general policy responsibility—and those in civic life, in the media and in the general public—will find these ideas useful. All these are, I know, concerned with the limited progress toward change and improvement. And they are ultimately the ones that will ensure the system changes.

As always with what I've written over the years, I invite your comments, criticisms and suggestions.

—Ted Kolderie
Saint Paul, Minnesota
June 2014

APPENDIX 1

System organization and system change

The Lure of Centralizing Authority

A core idea in this book is that de-centralized systems work better and change more easily. Here are two 'testimonials' in support of that case.

First are my notes of the discussion when Professor Charles Lindblom came to the Humphrey School of Public Affairs in 1988. Lindblom saw the impulse to 'take control of complex situations'—"The Allure of Order", as Jal Mehta later titled his history of education policy—as a serious problem in "the organization of human action".

Lindblom:

The reality is that most decision-making and planning proceeds through what I have called "disjointed incrementalism". Still, the human impulse is to try to take control of complex situations. And essentially there are two models, or approaches, through which people try to act.

One is coordination and change through centralized decision-making. Here information flows from the outlying parts of the organization into its center, and instructions flow back out.

The other is coordination and change through mutual adjustment. In this model information flows between and among the independent entities. You must note that this is not 'decentralization', which still implies a center. In the process of coordination through mutual adjustment there is no center; no single organization.

Our traditional theory is that coordination necessarily involves and requires a central mechanism. We all know real situations where coordination occurs without such a central mechanism. . . . Yet there remains a powerful bias in favor of the idea of central control.

Academics are trained to think centrally . . . to get a synoptic picture of "the whole problem". The challenge for them is to get an intellectual understanding of a situation in its entirety. This basic predisposition renders most academic people incapable of an objective view in the debate between central authority and mutual adjustment. Consultants, when called in to advise on the solution of a problem tend to take the same view. 'Comprehensive' planners do, as well.

Clearly, mutual adjustment . . . is the system in use at the world scale: the food system, the energy system, the materials-distribution system. So at the macro scale there is a phenomenally strong case for the use of this mechanism: coordination and control through mutual adjustment.

You might think that if an approach works well for the largest and most complex situations people would also use it for the smaller and less complex situations. What we find, however, is that at the micro level people are continually making great efforts to impose a system of centrality.

The process of what I have called mutual adjustment is messy and untidy, and is therefore unappealing to many persons. As a consequences the most logical and intelligent people tend to underrate its potential. This continues to be one of the major intellectual problems in the organization of human action.

The advantages of distributing authority

The other support comes in remarks by Ron Hubbs, then just retired from The Saint Paul Companies where during his years as CEO he had put through a decentralization of that big insurance firm. The occasion was a regional meeting of the Minnesota Association of School Administrators. Superintendents were troubled in the 1980s when school-based decision-making became a popular idea—with principals. Invited to defend the idea at a meeting of superintendents, I decided it might be a good idea to invite Hubbs to come with me. It was.

Hubbs:

You just can't beat a decentralized system. It gets closest to the level where the action really is. Education should have an advantage in moving into it, because your locations and your people are already physically dispersed.

Decentralization will not work unless you really delegate responsibility and authority. This means that the final decisions must be made at that lower level.

Two things stand in way of this working. One is that the people who now have the authority may not let go of it. The other is that the people at lower levels may not want to accept it. And, at the beginning some of these people may not be strong enough to handle it. But as they grow (and they will grow, with the responsibility) you can increase it. The process is not as difficult as it might sound. You start at the top, by asking "What is there that could be decided just as well by somebody other than me?" And then you keep working this question down the ladder. You really have to beware of the 'father knows best' attitude.

And it really does something for people. The executives are now essentially running businesses of their own. The company has confirmed their authority by making it very clear it will not let people dissatisfied with their decisions 'jump' over to the home office. Decisions are more rapid, too. Most of our company's new executives are coming up out of this system.

It avoids the evils of bureaucracy. Business is afflicted with this, just like government. When decisions have to go to the top it's not just a question of talking with the chief. His time is limited. So all kinds of other people up there . . . staff people . . . start to look at the question too. I've never been convinced that more people make a better decision. It's OK to say to one individual: "You make the decision, and I'll live with it".

Q: Let me give you an example that will show why some of us fear decentralization. In our district it resulted in our reading programs becoming different from school to school and within a school from grade to grade. Teachers were approaching it differently, so kids just weren't learning to read. It wasn't until we centralized the program and told teachers what materials they had to use that kids really began learn to read. Also, we had one principal who insisted on spending the capital money for new lockers rather than for micro-computers. We did not think we could permit people to make decisions we know are bad.

Hubbs: Performance is what counts. If the outcomes are bad you will have to do something about it. The people who work with an ineffective person are entitled to your attention to that kind of problem. But, again, it is important for the people who work for you to be given some idea ahead of time what is expected of them.

If there are some genuinely bad decisions it will reflect on the person who delegated the authority; no question about it. That's a risk you as the chief executive take. And it's a risk you have got to take. Sure, there will be times have to overrule somebody: No system of delegated authority will avoid this entirely. But if it begins to happen very often you've got a problem. Something is wrong with your system, which you'd better fix.

Don't be too afraid of bad decisions. There will be some of these. Individuals will be accountable for their record. The important thing is to get them to make decisions . . . One thing that seems to characterize people who get to the top is that along the way they were willing to risk their job for a decision they thought was right.

One of the problems, which decentralization aims to solve, is that the chief executive never has enough time to think about problems affecting the future of the operation. We are always in danger of being tied down by trivia. You have to find some arrangement that gives you time and the opportunity for the leadership that's really supposed to be your job.

APPENDIX 2

The problem of money and change

Once, 'money' was a principal strategy for change. Before 'standards' the basic idea was that change was possible only when financing was increased. That idea has now faded. I have not made 'money' a part of the theory of action I lay out in this book, believing it tends more to suppress than to promote change.

Still, some of the system changes, the institutional innovations, in public education have required adjustments in the system of K–12 finance. And of course, changes in the financial arrangements—such as to introduce support for early-childhood education—would involve action by state policymakers. So it might be useful to add a few notes here about changes in the policy about financing that might facilitate the development of a self-improving system.

1. Use common sense about the appeal for 'more'

The initial appeal from districts is often that change requires additional financing; that without more revenue, they cannot change. Clearly, those asked to provide the money need to understand how to respond to this appeal.

Never trade money for promises. Business and civic organizations—even occasionally governors—often sign on to help pass a larger appropriation or a levy increase in return for a promise from the district(s), or the system, to improve school and learning. This is a bad mistake. Getting improvement in the schools is not like buying a house, where the buyer pushes a check across the table and the seller delivers a deed in return. Districts cannot deliver improvement immediately. Improvement takes time. So the district essentially gives you an IOU; the improvement to be delivered later. If later it is not delivered, you're out of luck, have no recourse. So, do not trade money for promises. If you negotiate for change and improvement, identify the specific actions to be taken that clearly will produce change and improvement, make sure those actions are taken, then commit to the financing.

Is it really important if the district won't pay for it itself? A superintendent's standard approach is to say the district needs money in order to change and improve. That pitch is often made to foundations. When presented, foundations should ask the superintendent, "Is this important?" If the superintendent says, yes, it is important, then ask, "Is it *very* important?" If the answer to that is also 'yes', then ask, "Is it *very, very* important?" If the answer again is 'yes', then ask: "Now explain to me why, if it is that important, it isn't important enough for you to pay for yourself?"

Where does money matter? Distinguish between the things for which money matters and the things for which it does not. I remember Pam Costain, former chair of the Minneapolis Board of Education, being asked one day at a meeting of the discussion group on the Achievement Gap about the need for greater resources. "I'm a liberal Democrat", she said, "and I believe in public spending. But I have to tell you: the problems this district has are not the kind of problems that money solves".

2. Use money to leverage change

Periodically, districts come to the public—have to get a vote of approval—to borrow for capital purposes or to raise their tax levy. These occasions present an opportunity for organizations in the local 'civic system' to use their influence to correct weaknesses in the district's proposal or to get the district to do things it would not do without some pressure. A classic case occurred when the Minneapolis schools went to the voters in 1962 for the first district building program since the 1920s. Looking at the board's proposal, a local policy group, the Citizens League, saw it was a rehabilitation program, a few new rooms on every building in town—essentially a proposal designed to secure votes for the bond issue. Also, Minneapolis at that time had five high schools in a strip across the city south of downtown. The League urged the board to design a *replacement* program: closing whole buildings, selling those sites, building new schools at new sites. The board declined, went ahead with the vote. The League took the issue to the public, urging a 'no' vote. The measure was defeated. At the League's suggestion, the board then brought in a team from Michigan State—which recommended a replacement program. The capital plan was redone and resubmitted and with the League's support was approved. When the urban troubles came a few years later Minneapolis was building the newest high schools in the oldest parts of the city.

At other times, too, the League would condition its support on the board (or city council), committing itself *prior to the vote* that it would take this or that specific action. This kind of constructive pressure can be effective in a referendum.

Governors might try something similar, something different from what they normally do, when districts—individually or as a class—sue the state. Sometimes there are 'adequacy' suits, alleging the state is not providing 'enough'. Sometimes there are 'equity' suits, alleging unfairness to one set of districts or another. The impulse of the state's lawyer, the attorney general, is to deny the complaint. An astute governor, when sued, might use the suit as an opportunity for change—at least in states where the constitution requires the state to provide a "thorough and efficient" system of public education. The plaintiffs of course have in mind money as their relief, and a court presented with no alternative will likely accept that premise. A smart governor might tell the attorney general instead to *admit the complaint*— not with respect to money but with respect to the design of the K–12 system. 'Efficient' means "capable of accomplishing the result intended". Show that the K–12 system, as traditionally structured, is incapable of accomplishing the result intended. Lay out for the court a new arrangement that will turn K–12 into an effective system, a self-improving system.

3. Use state aids to finance choice

When the legislature 'withdraws the exclusive', takes down the old public-utility model of K–12, a question arises how the money follows the student moving from his/her 'home' district to the new district of attendance. This has been a puzzle for many states because school finance is most everywhere a combination of district revenue and state revenue.

Commonly, knowing the financing is a combination of revenue raised by local taxes and revenue raised by state taxes, people think that each student must be some combination of the two: part gold and part green. No; not necessarily.

A new way of thinking, the arrangement developed in Minnesota initially for inter-district open enrollment, might be of interest.

Minnesota said: Our equalized system first asks each district to pay a certain proportion of its wealth toward the cost of educating its children. Whatever that uniform rate raises in dollars—the amounts varying because of the differences in property valuation—the state will then pay the difference up to a level defined as full cost.

This makes it possible to think of a box of students, base-loaded with local dollars—all green, in effect—topped off with a layer (of whatever depth) of students fully state-paid, all gold.

A student moving from District A to District B is then a student 'off the top of the box'—all gold. So when the student moves, the state deducts the full per-pupil amount from District A and sends that full amount to District B.

The same approach is used in Minnesota to get revenue to the chartered public schools—with the exception of certain 'excess levy' revenues approved by local voters over and beyond the state-defined 'full cost'.

4. When discussing equity, talk about schools

The equity issue is usually raised by districts, often in lawsuits (see #2 above), arguing that the amount of revenue they get is 'not fair'. Often this appeal rests on their argument that their students, in the district as a whole, are needier. Less discussed is the question about equity as between 'needier' and 'not-needier' schools *within the district*.

In 1971, when Minnesota became the only state to re-equalize education finance through the political process, the legislation provided a 40 percent additional weighting on the formula for students from AFDC families. It was intended that this extra revenue would go to the schools that enrolled those students. In the event, the district kept the money, used it in other ways.

The reality is that senior—and therefore more expensive—teachers tend to accumulate in the schools with the less-disadvantaged children. The board pays salaries, so larger amounts go to those more-advantaged schools. If the district were to allocate revenue per-student, then—on the existing salary scale—the schools with the more-disadvantaged children would have more teachers and the more advantaged schools would have fewer. The politics involved mean that tends not to happen. This is a real issue, however. Press it.

5. Work to introduce incentives to use money differently

Districts definitely are *revenue*-maximizers. Whatever the level of spending, the appeal is for 'more'. *"Invest in Our Children"*, say the banners. "Money makes a difference", say the lawyers and policy advocates. To the question, 'How much?' there is never a clear response. People in Minnesota remember a lobbyist for one major K–12 association, asked to define 'enough', answering: "All you've got plus 10 percent". Essentially, as the head of another statewide K–12 association wrote in 2012, districts "spend all the money they can get their hands on". What drives expenditure is basically revenue-available.

For those who provide the money for the schools, elected officials and taxpayers, the goal must be to get out of this game. Their interest is in introducing incentives for districts and schools to make better use of the money they get. Chapter 11 contains some suggestions.

APPENDIX 3

Introducing Incentives

In the chapter about chartering and in the discussion about the importance of system-structure in K–12, there are references to "The States Will Have to Withdraw the Exclusive", the paper I wrote and circulated in the summer of 1990. Here are its early pages. Its latter part contained the proposal that appears in Chapter 3 for 'divestiture'.

THE STATES WILL HAVE TO WITHDRAW THE EXCLUSIVE

Seven years after the *Nation at Risk* report, this country still lacks a strategy for school improvement. We are serious about improvement. But we do not know how to make it happen.

In the first effort following the *Nation at Risk* report in 1983, we tried several things. We tried demonstrations in the hope that good practice would spread. We tried mandates. We tried money: real spending per pupil rose again in the 1980s after having risen by a quarter during the 1970s. Basically, we were trying to get better performance out of the existing schools. It was not a great success.

Out of it came the conclusion that, if student performance is to improve, the schools will have to be changed. More than this: radically changed.

And out of this conclusion has come the current effort at "re-structuring". Nobody quite knows exactly what it means. But at its core, there is a fairly coherent (and in a sense radical) vision: districts with professional teachers in "site-managed" schools, assessed and rewarded for the progress of the school in improving what students know and are able to do. This idea now dominates the conventional policy discussion about system-change and school-improvement.

But it is only a vision. It is not a strategy for action.

Institutions do not welcome change, especially radical change. They need a reason to change. And "re-structuring" does not give the district a reason to change. It assumes, as Jack Frymier put it in 1969, that "altruism is an adequate motivational base for change". It expects that boards, superintendents and teachers will do things they find personally difficult and institutionally unnecessary because these things are important for the country and good for kids.

This is not very realistic.

There have been some successes. There are important demonstrations in many schools. A number of districts have "re-structuring" contracts. There is now a state (Kentucky) in which the program will be tried state-wide. All of these are widely reported. The media create the impression of a changing system.

But change is more than getting words on paper, in contract or in law. Change must get established. It must last. And it must spread. The concern is that even in the most-noted "re-structuring districts" the implementation is proving—as the superintendent in Rochester, NY, Peter McWalters, said recently—"damned hard". In some districts, the educators do not want to use all the authority they are given. In others, the changes made might now be slipping away. The much-praised re-structuring in East Harlem, in New York City, has been in real jeopardy. Strenuous efforts by its friends may save it. But how many such defensive battles can be fought and won? For how long?

Above all, there is the problem of scale. This country has 40 million students and 2.2 million teachers in 84,000 schools in 15,000 districts. The problems are general—and serious. The change has got to be systemic. "Re-structuring" is simply not moving fast enough for the job that has to be done. Privately, there is real anxiety among those most committed to the cause.

"Re-structuring" improves on the old prescription: higher salaries, smaller classes and better training. But as it stands, it does not go to the heart of the problem. It is trying to persuade districts to change while accepting as given the arrangement of public education that makes it hard for them to change. This makes no basic sense. We need a new approach. We need to examine the givens of the arrangement, find what makes it so hard to change, and change *that*.

Why Education Resists Change

The critical given is the idea of districting itself. The state does not deal with schools; it deals with districts. Legally, schools do not exist; districts exist. The district is defined by its boundaries. These create an area in which there is one and only one organization offering public education, to whose schools the students who live in that area are assigned. Public education is organized as a pattern of territorial exclusive franchises.

That exclusive franchise is the heart of the problem.

» It means the state agrees the district will have the final decision about improvement. Governors and legislators like to talk as if they control improvement. They don't. They can propose and promise, plead and threaten. They can give money. They can issue orders. And often, the districts do respond. But whether they do or not in the end is up to them. If the district does not give the students a good education the state does not send in another organization that will. It accepts the pace of improvement at which the district is able or willing to move.

» The state also agrees to accept whatever reasons the district has for its decision to change or not to change, even if those reasons have to do mainly with the private and personal interests of the adults involved, as they sometimes do.

» And the state agrees to accept those decisions and the reasons for them, whether or not the students learn. Within very broad limits, the state assures the districts their material success—their existence, their students, their revenues, everything except their annual increases—independent of the level of student success.

Nobody should wonder why in public education "the cards are stacked against innovation". An organization with that exclusive franchise feels no need to change.

David K. Cohen put it gently when he wrote in 1986 that education contains "weak incentives for the introduction of innovations that would cause internal stress". And proposals for radical change surely do cause internal stress. Change disrupts settled routines. It upsets people. It causes controversy. It threatens the real interests of powerful organizations.

As they consider proposals for change, the superintendent, board, principal, union and teachers weigh the potential benefits to the students against the risk of creating "internal stress". They want to help the kids. But upsetting people might cause controversy. It might produce a grievance. It might lose an election. It might cause a strike. It might damage a career.

The risks are real. There is nothing countervailing, nothing that requires students' interests to be put first, nothing very bad that will happen if the decision is to say no. As things stand, a no is the end of the matter: The principal who wants to change has nowhere else to go, the teacher has nowhere else to go, parents and students have nowhere else to go.

There is almost nothing anyone can change without getting someone else's permission. Yet almost everyone has the power to check everyone else.

And practically nothing depends on making the improvements for which the public is pressing: clear objectives, measurement of performance, new technology or better learning methods.

Unless something quite unusual happens, the students and the revenues will be there anyway. Good educators tell their colleagues, "We have to change". But that is not true in any real sense. They do not have to.

The students get what altruism, courage and the random appearance of exceptional individuals provide in the way of improvement—which is often a lot. But the system puts them second. The system puts adults first. As Albert Shanker told the Itasca Seminar in Minnesota in 1988: "This is a system that can take its customers for granted".

Why the State Will Have to Act

For a country serious about improvement, this is an absurd arrangement. We can hardly expect the district to do the hard things involved in change if we guarantee it its success whether it does these things or not.

This unproductive situation is not the educators' doing. The system is not one they created. Many might like to see it changed. Ted Sizer remarks near the end of *Horace's Compromise* that "the people are better than the system". That's true. The people are as good as any. They are working in a bad system.

It is time to say this: our system of public education is a bad system. It is terribly inequitable. It does not meet the nation's needs. It exploits teachers' altruism. It hurts kids.

We ought to change it. It is unproductive and unfair to put people under incentives that are not aligned with the mission they have been given to perform. That leads to blaming the people for failures that are the fault of the system . . . and we are now deeply into blaming people for the failures of public education. Parents blame teachers and administrators. Educators in response blame parents, and kids. It is all wrong. We should stop blaming people. We should fix the system.

We can do this. We do not have to take the system as given. The system is a policy-construct.

But to change it, we will have to go beyond the district. "We can never turn around enough districts," ECS president Frank Newman said in a "Statehouse to Schoolhouse" discussion, "without changing the incentives in the system".

Changing incentives means providing reasons and opportunities for people to do in their own interest and on their own initiative the "stressful" things that change requires. Changing incentives in the system means re-structuring the environment in which districts live.

It means withdrawing their exclusive franchise.

Only the state can do this. The districting is in state law. The responsibility for action rests with the legislatures, and with the governors whose proposals often begin the legislative process.

The state's job is not to run the schools. The state's job is to provide a workable system for those who do. It owes boards, administrators and teachers—and the public—a system in which those who do change and improve are supported and rewarded, and in which those who do not are the ones put at risk.

Everywhere in this country the state is in default on that obligation.